DESIGNING·WITH
FLOWERS

DESIGNING WITH
FLOWERS

Tricia Guild

Photography by David Montgomery/Text by Nonie Niesewand

MITCHELL BEAZLEY

DESIGNING WITH FLOWERS
Tricia Guild

Edited and designed by Mitchell Beazley International Ltd,
Artists House, 14–15 Manette Street, London W1V 5LB

Executive Art Editor **Jacqui Small**   Executive Editor **Robert Saxton**
Assistant Editor **Susan Mitchell**
Assistant Art Editor on the Flower Directory **Prue Bucknall**
Horticultural consultant **Caroline Boisset**, B.Sc. (Hons) Hort., M.Sc., M.I.Hort.
Production **Philip Collyer**
Illustration **Niki Kemball, Sally Launder** and **Josephine Martin**

Reprinted 1988, 1989
Grateful acknowledgment is made to Michael Joseph Ltd
for permission to quote from *Vita Sackville-West's Garden Book* (1968).
Lines from the poem 'The Garden' by Vita Sackville-West
reproduced by permission of Curtis Brown Ltd
on behalf of the author's Estate.

ISBN 0 85533 591 2

Typeset by Servis Filmsetting Ltd, Manchester
Colour reproduction by Gilchrist Brothers Ltd, Leeds
Printed by Koninklijke Smeets Offset b.v., Weert, Netherlands

CONTENTS

INTRODUCTION

I can think of nothing that brings a room alive more immediately than flowers do. Nor anything that offers us a more spontaneous means of arranging the different areas we live in with greater interest and imagination. Sensitively arranged, cut flowers can transform and continually refresh interiors with their natural beauty.

Some arrangements, of course, look decidedly *un*natural – especially those that use wire, blocks of foam or other devices to imprison the living flowers in rigidly contrived designs. Such distortions are to my mind the very opposite of creative flower design. The aim should be not to draw attention to human ingenuity but to do justice to the individual characteristics of each plant as it grows outdoors. However much time and care you put into a composition, the final result should look natural, unaffected, inevitable. Such apparently artless effects can be achieved just as well with florists' flowers as with cuttings from your own garden or window box.

Colour, line, form, texture, scale and scent are all aspects that you need to consider when planning an arrangement. If this list makes flower design sound rather technical, I hope this book will soon dispel such an impression. The main thing is to trust in the evidence of your own eyes. There are basic principles to follow, but the ultimate yardstick is your own sense of what looks balanced and pleasing. As you become more experienced, you will be able to apply these principles instinctively.

Composition – the art of combining flowers, foliage and container to make a design that pleases the eye – is too often considered in isolation. There is another dimension to flower arranging, and that is the relationship between flowers and their surroundings. It is a cornerstone of my philosophy as a designer that flowers should be chosen and grouped to complement the general impact of the decoration. In other words, flowers are as much a part of interior design as wallpaper, fabrics or furniture. If you use flowers to echo, or deliberately contrast with, the colours, patterns or textures of your decorative scheme, they will help to give new life to your surroundings.

The section on "Interiors" shows how I have tried to apply this principle in various homes (including my own), using flowers to sustain an overall style or mood, or to create unexpected contrast. There is often an element of calculated surprise in my arrangements – lavish bouquets of exotic blooms in homely settings, simple nosegays of country garden flowers in grand, formal rooms.

If, after looking at this book, you seek a further source of inspiration for flower arrangements, visit if you can the famous English country garden at Sissinghurst in Kent, started in 1930 by Vita Sackville-West. To me, this is the most beautiful of gardens. I appreciate it in particular for its superb treatment of colour: delightful drifts of harmonizing hues are offset in places by startling contrasts.

In designing with flowers, visual inspiration is worth far more than dogma. If this book conveys something of my own love for flowers it will be thanks in large measure to the photographs of David Montgomery, who has interpreted my arrangements with skill and sensitivity. Like myself, he believes in letting flowers make their own glorious statement.

Tricia Guild.

COLOUR

With any flower, you notice colour first, then scent, then texture. The way that flowers look when grouped in various colour combinations is the beginning of creative flower design.

Victorian gardeners favoured bedding plants in strict regiments of garishly contrasting hues. It was the English gardener Gertrude Jekyll who took garden design toward a more informal, harmonizing style, and this is the approach favoured today in cut flower arrangements. Contrasts, of course, have an important part in flower compositions, but they need to be handled with sensitivity.

The following section of the book begins with some basic principles of colour composition, and goes on to describe the floral palette hue by hue, with many inspiring suggestions for specific colour partnerships.

A controlled mix of pale pastels in a country garden assortment. *Stephanandra* leaf sprays, snippets of golden privet and white *Lilium regale* are set among the blues of cornflowers, love-in-a-mist and delphiniums, mauve scabious and sweet peas and a single deep pink hydrangea. Toning different shades of mauve, pink and blue created a harmonious colour composition, anchored firmly in four all-white jugs. With so many different colours and forms in the flowers, the echoing containers are needed to unify the arrangement: a collection of patterned jugs would have been too emphatic.

HARMONIZING COLOURS

Vita Sackville-West tellingly compared gardening with painting: "One has the illusion of being an artist painting a picture – putting a dash of colour here, taking out another dash of colour there, until the whole composition is to one's liking." But whereas the gardener has to anticipate effects on a long time-scale, the designer of an indoor garden of cut flowers can see instantly how the colours react together: all you do is take a bunch, set it in a vase, stand back and observe the effect. If necessary, you can take out colours that offend, break up drifts of the same colour with leaves or flowers of a different hue, or inject sharp contrast.

The colours in a flower arrangement should always be chosen to complement their surroundings – the wall coverings, drapes, furnishings and paintwork. This theme is treated in depth in a later section of this book. But as a first step, you need to learn the basic palette of flowers and the various ways in which you can combine colours, in controlled proportions, for specific effects.

Combining colours successfully is a basic skill that needs to be acquired. First, there is the art of harmonizing colours – that is, choosing colours from within the same area of the spectrum, so that each colour appears to drift or blend harmoniously into its neighbour. Some designers find it helpful to visualize a "colour wheel" in which all the hues of the spectrum are arranged continuously in a circle; harmonizing colours are adjacent to each other on the wheel, while vividly contrasting colours ("complementaries") are opposite each other. The seven basic colours are red, orange, yellow, green, blue, indigo and violet, but of course there are countless tones and shades.

The other technique is to create an unexpected contrast by putting opposites from the colour wheel against each other. A contrasting splash of colour – what decorators call an "accent" colour – can make a strong impact in an otherwise harmonious arrangement. For example, among pastel hues you could add a single vivid bloom of lime-green *Helleborus corsicus* or green-tinged white guelder rose: the effect would be to bring the harmonizing colours even closer together.

Colours are either warm or cool.

The warm colours, which contain yellow pigment, include scarlet, orange, yellow-greens (such as lime green and lettuce green) and yellow itself; the cool range, containing blue pigment, includes crimson, violet, indigo and blue-green – for example, the blue of eucalyptus or olive leaves – as well as blue. If you combine colours within these groups, they will appear to flow into each other, without any jarring effect. But if you set, for example, scarlet against crimson, you will create a contrast.

Harmonizing colours are much easier to combine successfully than are contrasting colours. The simplest approach is to choose flowers from the same family or species. Stocks, for example, bloom in cream, soft pink, lilac and mauve, all of which combine sympathetically. Common lilac offers a profusion of violet, lilac and white flowers on generously sized sprays. There are also the variations on blue found in delphiniums, and the golds and bronzes of chrysanthemums.

Once you have chosen the basic colour scheme, you can deepen the effect by adding darker shades of the same hues, or lighten it by adding paler tints, or white or cream. Group paler colours together to give them emphasis, and use foliage to heighten or subdue the impact of more vivid blooms. All colours look more brilliant beside grey foliage: the leaves of senecio, for example, will bring out even the palest hue. The purple leaves of weigela or purple sage, on the other hand, will dampen the more brilliant colours.

To some extent, colours change according to the seasons. White and yellow flowers herald the spring, followed by the blues of bluebells, iris, grape hyacinths and lilacs. In mid summer, when annuals bloom in every colour imaginable, more skill is needed to achieve a harmonizing effect. Autumn brings the russet tones of leaves and berries and the tawny late-summer flowerings of chrysanthemum and dahlias. You can complement these seasonal flowers with florist's flowers.

Harmonizing colours are those that are naturally related to each other by a shared pigment. Yellow and orange are close enough to each other on the spectrum to make a pleasing harmony. In this springtime assembly, the orange edging on the cream and white narcissi picks up the yellow of the daffodils and the right-hand container.

These pink, blue and purple drifts of colour, gliding into each other, are made up of agapanthus, phlox, acanthus and delphiniums. The bright green bells of Ireland, which add a dash of accent colour, are placed in a separate container to concentrate and localize their effect. The container colours contribute to the overall impression.

CONTRASTING COLOURS

Contrasting colours demand an assured touch, especially if you are bunching flowers on a large scale. Random seedings often produce spectacular colour contrasts outdoors, but such effects will seem excessive in an interior. Indoors, contrasts should be handled boldy but not brazenly.

The colours that are opposite each other on the colour wheel make the strongest contrasts – green with red, blue with yellow, for example. When blue is combined with its near-relative purple the result is a soothing harmony, but pair blue with lemon, its opposite on the colour wheel, and the impact is much more eye-catching: each contrasting hue intensifies the other.

Violet and orange is another vivid contrast. The French Impressionist Claude Monet painted this dramatic contrast in his garden at Giverny – orange nasturtiums tumbling in front of banked violet-blue aster. Indoors, mass these hues in bold sweeps: they are not colours for a hesitant touch.

The intensity of each colour in the contrasting pair is an important consideration. Hues of identical density will war with each other. It is by far preferable to combine a light with a dark colour, or a strong tone with a muted one. Proportion and form are also key factors. Orange sunflowers pooled with purple pansies would be an unfortunate partnership: the giant sunflowers would dwarf the pansies, and the colours, as much as the scale, would compete. However, lavender spikes among Iceland poppies, or the orange ruffles of hollyhock spires placed among tall stalks of

Anemones in purple, magenta and pink and white harmonize with dotted pink gypsophila. The dominant impression here is of the contrast of purple and pink flowers in a green vase – a counterpoint echoed on a smaller scale by the purple ribbon and old volume. There is also the contrast of dark green leaves with the black centres of the anemones.

Right: **This close-up shows blue delphiniums accented with a grey bud of whitebeam (*Sorbus aria*). The icegreen guelder rose makes a vivid focal point in an otherwise harmonizing bunch.**

mauve Canterbury bells, would complement each other well in form and tone.

If one of the colours in a contrasting arrangement is broken up into a pattern, its brilliance is reduced. You can observe this with variegated foliage or with the old-fashioned rose 'Rosa Mundi', whose pink petals are splashed with white. Emphasize such variegations by adding plain blooms in each colour of the pair – for example, you could make a dramatic contrast using 'Rosa Mundi' with the roses coloured in the purple-pink of 'Cardinal de Richelieu', the crimson-maroon of 'William Lobb' and the white

'Iceberg', all in a white porcelain bowl.

Harmonizing colour works very well in large bunches, but contrasting colours tend to be more successful on a smaller scale. For example, you could make a vivid nosegay by mingling hot pink nerines, yellow daffodils, deeply crimson parrot tulips and black-centred purple anemones. Another approach is to create a graduated contrast, with a drift of blending colours between each of the two extremes. Or again, you could add zest to a harmonizing bunch with a small vivid accent in a contrasting hue – an effect comparable to the use of contrasting piping on a sofa.

Yellowy greens contrast with blue, whereas blue-greens obviously harmonize. Here, bluebells and borage are placed against lime-green _Helleborus foetidus_ and greeny yellow _Euphorbia robbiae_. The vivid contrast is exaggerated by the bright blue markings on the container. In the left-hand vase a handful of red delphinium buds magnetizes our attention: this is really the hub of the whole composition.

THE GLEAM OF WHITE

White is the colour of so many beautiful flowers – waxy white gardenia, luminously glowing moon flowers, hazy white flowers of midsummer gypsophila, white fragrant jasmine (characteristically clustering against a grey stone wall), and the velvety white of the scented tobacco plant, *Nicotiana*, that gleams so exquisitely at night.

The look of white petals varies according to their texture, as well as the markings on the petals. Delicate veining in pink, gold and bronze will also influence the overall effect. Look, for example, at the Madonna lily which grows so freely in cottage gardens: its inner trumpet is beautifully suffused with gold. Or look at the golden markings on the white flag iris. Such subtle differences enable you to achieve a variety of moods with white flowers, even in monochrome displays.

White can tone down a mixed bunch, or give added zest to an otherwise one-colour arrangement. More boldy, you can take the lead with white, using it as the main theme.

Arum lilies, spiralled here in a glass cylinder, are among the few flowers that are pure white. The petals are beautifully textured and veined, like fine paper. Notice how the dark green spathes of the lilies emphasize their whiteness. I added tuberoses to bring scent to this simple, strong display.

White blooms and silver-leafed plants enrich each other, and white-and-green variegated leaves also make excellent accompaniments – for example, stripy *Hosta fortunei* or spotted *Pulmonaria*. Mix these leaves with a few white roses, white lilac, sweet rocket, stocks and white viola, and you will have an informal, fragrant, all-white bunch in no way reminiscent of a bridal bouquet.

White flowers bloom throughout the year. Pale, wintry landscapes produce the finest white flowers – snowdrops, miniature iris, hyacinth, crocus and jonquil. Florists improve on seasonal effects by forcing spring bulbs under glass, so the plants often grow with incredibly long stems as they reach for the light to bloom. Use these stems to best advantage in glass containers so that the length and slenderness of each stalk can be admired. Other offerings of spring include bare boughs arching with pear and cherry blossom, which you can bring indoors in great branches to fill a room with the promise of summer.

As summer approaches, white flowers are often scented, beginning with the lily of the valley, then white lilacs, the tobacco flower, the Mexican orange and the mock orange. Late summer produces the cheerful white snapdragon, as well as daisies and asters whose sunny yellow-centred flowers go well with variegated golden leaves.

In woodlands, starry white anemones and delicate violas carpet shady walks. Likewise, you can brighten up a shady place at home with white flowers set among dark glossy leaves.

Vita Sackville-West was passionately fond of white flowers: "I love colour and rejoice in it," she wrote, "but white is lovely for me forever." She went on to rhapsodize about the delicious shades white flowers can take on in twilit or moonlit gardens. By cutting white flowers for home arrangements you can enjoy such mysteries of light equally well indoors.

Right: **A more casual array of white flowers, on a smaller scale. Bells of lily of the valley are defined by the lime-green *Euphorbia robbiae* and *Helleborus foetidus*. The green leaves that sheath the lily of the valley as it grows encircle the arrangement protectively in a regular pattern.**

THE ELEGANCE OF CREAM

This florist's rose, 'Landia', is many-petalled, sweet-scented and richly creamy, as though the golden centre had lightly stained the veined petals. The bloom was of such singular beauty that I used it alone, as a table centrepiece.

Larger than a rose, the cream peony has a voluminous quality. Here, the buttery glow of its petals is intensified by the white vase. Fresh green sprigs of young beech balance the celadon green vase and add a sense of fresh-picked immediacy to the longer-lasting peonies of mid summer.

Most popular decorating colour for neutral backgrounds is that ubiquitous paint colour called "magnolia" – a misnomer, as it does not have the rare sheen of its floral namesake, *Magnolia grandiflora*. It is this sheen that makes cream flowers beautiful. Each petal has its own rich texture that no uniform application of paint can hope to reproduce. Just as the shine on a damson enriches its purple-crimson, so the buttery sheen of cream flowers gives them their distinctive character differentiating them from white.

With cream-coloured roses in particular, it sometimes seems as though the golden heart of the flowers has lightly stained the petals from the centre. Gaze into the fragrant depths of roses to see the colour gradu-ations within the layered petals. The old-fashioned rose, *Rosa* 'Alba Maxi-ma', known as the Jacobite rose, has double white petals flushed at the centre with cream. Hybrids like 'Penelope' have soup-plate-sized creamy flowers with soft golden centres. While gardeners today scoff at these hybrids, preferring the old-fashioned varieties, flower arrangers today cannot afford such indulgences, since old roses have old-fashioned flowering habits, blooming only once in early summer. By contrast, 'Penelope' will freely flower through early to late summer, providing creamy blooms in such profusion that you can cut them and use them extravagantly in throw-away gestures. Set single heads among specially selected props. Old books, finely bound in vellum, or old music scores, are appropriate back-grounds for 'Penelope's' creamy papery petals.

A single cream rose set beside a bowl of aromatic, dappled potpourri will emphasize both the bloom and fragrance of the fresh flower. At the dinner table, a single magnolia laid on each white porcelain plate beside a white damask napkin completes an attractive formal setting, as well as offering an amusing buttonhole for each guest.

A flamboyant, albeit inedible, cream table centrepiece can be grown from seeds: the creamy minia-ture waterlily (*Nymphaea pygmea helvolva*), scaled down in size for people without pools to grow indoors. This diminutive waterlily was once a popular decorative motif, as impor-tant to Art Nouveau as the pome-granate was to the Renaissance or the rose to the Rococo style. To grow your own, you need a container one foot across and seven inches deep – for example, a glass salad bowl. A copper pan would have the advan-tage of disguising the tangle of roots beneath the lily pads. Slash the seeds across, then immerse them in water maintained at around 75°F (24°C), changing the hot water twice daily until germination takes place in a month or so. If this seems a lot of bother, it is nothing beside the efforts of 19th-century horticulturists to in-troduce this beautiful jungle exotic to northern climes.

THE SUNSHINE GLOW OF YELLOW

Yellow has the power to dazzle. In this display, gleaming yellow mimosa with its feathery foliage, together with flower heads of yarrow, are in harmony with a scrubbed pine container and a simple woven mat. All the yellows here have the same value, sharpened by the delicate green foliage that surrounds them. A few geranium leaves were added to bring a fresh citric scent to the aromatic mimosa.

Gold or yellow blooms are always glittering, never dull. The sunflower radiates vitality in its sunburst shape. But equally cheerful are yellow flowers that come in less symbolic forms – the yellow trumpets of the day lily, or clusters of fluffy mimosa. Plumes of golden rod and spires of yellow snapdragon seem to reflect the lengthening rays of afternoon sun. Such clear yellows can fill a room with summery brightness. The great English gardener Gertrude Jekyll remarked that to enter a garden of gold flowers even on the greyest day is like coming unexpectedly into sunshine.

Primroses and daffodils can herald springtime. Later come mimosa, sprigs of lemony dogwood, yellow shrub roses and flag irises and, in later summer, St John's wort. A welcome source of early-winter yellow is the winter jasmine, whose sweet fragrance becomes stronger indoors. Late-winter wallflowers have a strong scent in a warm room – a mix of jasmine and citron.

Variegated green-and-yellow foliage is invaluable for harmoniously patterned compositions. Suitable ingredients for dappled effects are variegated hollies, hostas, ivies and dogwood. From deciduous trees in autumn it is worth collecting pale yellow leaves before they fall, to create a mellow mood with more than a hint of the year's close.

Yellows contrast well with violets and purples – their complementaries in the spectrum. As one of many variations on this theme, try combining pale yellow primroses with sprigs of weigela and purple-leaved clippings of the smoke tree (*Cotinus coggygria* 'Foliis Purpureis'). A posy using a more restricted palette can be made from 'Harvest Moon' carnations, dark-eyed rudbeckia, sunny marigolds and russet Peruvian lilies; to bind the arrangement use evergreen leaves, variegated ivy and lime-green leaves of the tobacco plant.

Another approach is to use a single yellow flower as an accent in an assorted bunch. The yellow will seem to advance, instantly attracting the eye. ("Advancing colours" is a designer's term, for the warm palette of red, orange and yellow which seem to bring the surface nearer.) The gleam of a golden lily makes an effective focal point when used in this way.

Both the Californian poppy and the Iceland poppy have a range of yellow blooms from yellow to gold. With all poppies, you should cut the flower before the bud opens and plunge the cut stem into boiling water for 30 seconds: this helps the flower to last and accelerates the unfurling of the bud. The Californian poppy is a true sun-worshipper and will shut its petals at night to open again at dawn.

You can heighten the impact of yellow flowers by a careful choice of backgrounds or containers. This colour has a particular affinity with mellow brick, stone, wood panelling, terracotta and wickerwork.

The most predictable treatment for cut daffodils is to display them in great bunches. However, a few yellow trumpets among white narcissi can look as bold as any massed display. Here, the yellow is sharpened by a single green guelder rose to create a dual accent of bright colour among the frosty white early spring flowers.

THE BLUSH OF APRICOT

Two apricot roses flank a peachy-pink rose, whose petals are edged with pure pink. A single white *regale* lily with yellow markings heightens the golden glow. Green leaves, on the other hand, would have a dampening effect.

Between pink and yellow there is a range of colours to which we give fruit names. Peach has a pink tinge, apricot is suffused with orange, while mango is a mix of orange and pink.

Relatively few flowers have these hues, the most familiar being roses and gladioli. Floribunda roses, which bloom from summer to mid autumn, may have sumptuous mountains of peach or apricot petals: there is 'Alison Wheatcroft' in apricot-pink and 'Fritz Nobis' with soft salmon-pink flowers that darken at their centres. Gladiolus, popular in Art Deco interiors in the 1930s, is poised for a revival of interest. It yields large summer flowers of pale orange-pink ('Peter Pears') or a bolder apricot flecked with crimson ('Toulouse Lautrec'). The smaller *Gladiolus nanus*, which flowers earlier, from mid spring, offers 'Spitfire' in salmon-orange and 'Spring Glory' in salmon-pink.

Because of their novelty value, peach and apricot blooms make a dramatic impact in monochrome arrangements. Warm, peaceful colours, they demand neither contrasts nor harmonies. An effective method is to use a single bloom in a stem vase: an apt choice for a modern apartment would be a gerbera daisy, whose graphic good looks and unusual colour make a strong statement. To temper the effect, use cream flowers as an accompaniment, or a frame of small white flowers to add distinction.

Some flowers bloom in a whole range of warm colours: Iceland poppies, for example, have peach, apricot, salmon, coral and lemon-yellow.

Various combinations are sometimes found on the same plant – and certainly all these hues can be produced from the same seed packet. A bunch of these mixed colours, all with the same tissue-paper delicacy, would work well, without jarring. But when you mix species, more care is required. A single peach-coloured poppy placed with yellow marguerites would fail disastrously, the yellow of the open-faced daisies being much too bold for the subtle peach. Take this as a general rule: when choosing pinks or yellows to go with peach, be sure to avoid the more clamorous shades.

Hollyhocks are a family in which great spires of peach-coloured blooms are to be found among the more common pink and yellow flowers. A mixed group in a simple stoneware crock, such as an old mustard jar, can look beautifully harmonious.

The complementary colour to peach is slate-blue. This is rarely found in flowers, although the puffs of ageratum, the floss flower, in the steely-blue variety 'Baltic', contrast with peach; they have the same delicate texture and hue. Some blue-green leaves can mix with peach flowers – for example, the silvery *Artemisia* 'Powys Castle' and the gunmetal cider gum (*Eucalyptus gunnii*).

Pewter makes a good container for peach and apricot flowers especially when silver-grey foliage is used as a back-up. Its dull sheen provides the perfect foil in the composition.

A simple, almost minimalist, arrangement encourages us to gaze into the open face of this gerbera, or Transvaal daisy, to admire the novelty of its colour. Not so bright as orange, nor so clear as yellow, apricot flowers deserve individual treatment. To set off the beauty of this bloom I accompanied it with *Hosta fortunei* leaves and a stem of young beech.

THE BLAZE OF ORANGE

Never pale or peaceful, orange is an attention-getter, even when mixed in different shades. Its vibrant glow causes the eye to refocus, optically foreshortening distance, so that the colour appears to leap forward.

On the colour spectrum, the complementary of orange is violet blue. Juxtaposing the two creates a vivid contrast that makes both colours seem luminous. Tread carefully when choosing a complementary pairing; some hues, such as the pale violet of lavender, clash disturbingly with orange. Gertrude Jekyll recommended planting some orange lilies (*Lilium bulbiferum croceum*) alongside blue delphiniums to enhance the brilliance of both colours. Indoors, you could tint and shade these two complementaries by adding berberis in a deeper violet than the delphinium blues and tawny chrysanthemums to the orange lilies.

Using drifts of graduated colour you can extend orange through the sunset hues into dusky violet by adding the purple foliage of the textured purple sage.

Avoid combining autumn leaves with orange flowers: the effect can be overpowering. Instead, temper orange flowers with a green or silver-grey leafy framework.

Whoever said that nature makes no mistakes in colour harmony was either "colour-blind or a sentimentalist"; thus remarked Vita Sackville-

Individual blooms of ranunculus spring from this cluster of small earthenware pots. There is citric yellow, white and a single vivid pink as an accent colour, but the orange dominates, its glowing boldness highlighted by leaves of tolmiea in apple green.

West. She singled out the orange blooms of *Alstroemeria* Ligtu hybrids, randomly seeded alongside rose-pink alstroemeria in an unsatisfactory combination. Yellow-oranges are demanding colours, and usually need to be soothed, not emphasized with a mass of pink. Separate orange and pink with leaves or white flowers, or alternatively use a single pink as a colour accent.

Wallflowers grow together in a harmony of tawny gold, russet, mahogany, yellow and orange. Another early source of orange flowers is the barberry (*Berberis darwinii*). Narcissi combine yellows and oranges well, while later in the season there is marigold, the orange day lily, *Lilium henryi*, *Lilium canadense*, Iceland poppies, the flecked orange tiger lily, and the sunflower and nasturtium, the latter tumbling in orange, red and gold over its scalloped leaves.

As autumn progresses, the orange-yellow fruits of the spindle tree split to reveal scarlet seeds, and rose hips produce delightful clusters of orange-red berries.

In a shaft of light, orange montbretia rises above geranium leaves. The flower and the leaves both share the same yellow pigment. Imagine yew in place of geranium – the orange would blaze with intense colour in contrast to the dark evergreen. But this arrangement harmonizes with a luminous, sunny brightness. The clear green cube container and two white ceramic pots enhance the subtlety of the mix.

THE WARMTH OF RED

Red can be double trouble for flower arrangers striving to harmonize colours. There are two principle groups, crimson and vermilion, and mixing the two in equal proportions can be disastrous, as they will war with each other. Crimson – that is, deep red tinged with blue – belongs with carmine and magenta; vermilion, which leans toward orange, includes cinnabar and scarlet. Using red successfully in a mixed bunch depends upon picking the right shade – either blue-tinged or yellow-tinged – to go with the other colours in the group.

A monochrome arrangement of reds can be enlivened by adding a contrasting shade of red as an accent. A dozen red roses may be a declaration of an admirer, but it says more about your style if you add to the display a jolt of creamy pink roses or the splashed crimson-and-white 'Rosa Mundi'.

Employing red in arrangements takes both confidence and tact. Whether the colour reigns supreme in single-stem vases or contrasts with other hues in a mixed bunch, red will always hold the eye. It is easier by far to combine a vibrant red with a restrained hue than with another of equal strength. Nevertheless, a brilliant and fearless pairing can look stunningly beautiful if you get it right.

With the spring-flowering crimsons of the *Camellia japonica* 'Mathotiana Rubra', cyclamen, anemones or flowering crab apple, deep-purple foliage makes a rich accompaniment – for example, the velvet-textured leaves of sage, purple basil or weigela. The crab apple 'Eleyi', which has crimson flowers and purple leaves, will give you an idea of how nature pairs these colours.

Later in the season, vermilion tulips, carnations, geraniums, snapdragons, poppies and peonies can be teamed with silver-grey foliage from artemisia, stachys or artichokes. (Grey will not alter adjacent hues,

only intensify them.)

As summer progresses, the reds hot up. The hot, bright colours of dahlias or geraniums seem to advance out of their background – an effect you can emphasize by choosing dark-green leaves, which will make the reds glow like jewels. Gardeners use a similar trick when they plant deep-red flowers adjacent to dark hedges of yew.

Only a few blooms are red in this many-coloured bunch of ranunculus, yet they dominate the overall effect. Their brazen scarlet is emphasized by central placing, and the bright contrast of *Hosta fortunei* leaves – green is directly opposite red on the colour wheel. With flowers that spill their petals, fill a shallow bowl with scented water – a few drops of rosewater or potpourri freshener will suffice – to catch them as they tumble.

Right: **Red is an advancing colour: it never retires shyly in a corner. Here, red roses are boldy keyed in to match a crimson pail set casually on some open stairs. The reds are full-strength, undiluted by the white and pink roses in the same bunch. This is the bluish red of crimson – quite different from the yellow red of scarlet, or the vermilion of poinsettia.**

THE VIBRANCY OF PINK

Pink can be close to yellow in the salmon-pink range or to blue in the mauvey pinks. Take the foxglove. This is most commonly seen in gardens and hedgerows as a pink flower with a blue tinge. But in the cultivar 'Sultan's Apricot', the foxglove is flushed with apricot as the name suggests, and in a mixed bunch needs back-up from yellow-toned flowers.

Hot pinks that edge toward orange go well with the fresh brightness of lime-green leaves, whereas dark green leaves make pale pinks look redder. You can watch this principle at work on a rosy-cheeked apple, whose pink tinges deepen where they meet the surrounding green.

The cool pinks that are linked with blue pigments blend with mauve and purple, like heather on a misty moorland, or sweet peas on a summer day. Less emphatic, these cool pinks evoke the cottage garden, since many of the oldest species are

Pink can be toned down to a pastel with grey foliage and creamy white blooms, or alternatively it can be sharpened with green. Here, single sprays of pink foxgloves with *Astrantia* and *Hosta fortunei* leaves are brightened with yellowish-green heads of dill.

pink – from roses to carnations. Pale spring blossom, the watermelon pink of the poppy *Papaver orientale* 'Sultana', the shell-pink translucence of the peony *Paeonia* 'Janice', or the pink blush of the Bourbon rose 'Madame Pierre Oger', all belong within this range.

Early-flowering cherry blossom and pink camellias are followed by roses, peonies, poppies, lilies, the nerine that lasts so well in water, and the late-flowering amaryllis, or Belladonna lily. Lacecap hydrangeas that turn pink in an alkaline soil and mountainous froths of pink rhododendron can be cut in great armfuls to make a bold indoor display. Pink is a particularly good colour to use in high summer, with the hot colours that dominate our gardens.

Be adventurous with pink. Two scarlet climber roses mark the entrance to the pink and mauve garden at Sissinghurst Castle. It took courage to plant scarlet against the pink background; even the walls of the Tudor castle are pink – the colour of "raspberry fool" as Vita Sackville-West remarked. With cut flowers creative combinations like this will not have such long-lasting effects. Fuchsia delicately combines pink with scarlet, but for a similar effect you could use roses, carefully chosen to match the fuchsia's tones.

When mixing different pinks, keep the tones closely related and use foliage to heighten or deepen the effect. Pale pinks massed together tend to lose definition, so copy nature and give them a ruff of dark green leaves. Grey foliage highlights pink particularly well – for example, anthemis, senecio or lavender-cotton. Or deepen the pink with purplish sage, feathery purple fennel or plum-coloured weigela leaves. To prevent pink from seeming claustrophobic, use a single accent colour – for example, you could create an arrangement in which spurge cuts through a mass of pink rhododendrons.

Pure pink peonies are highlighted in this arrangement with the dark green of hostas and a glimpse of the grey-green underside of artichoke leaves. Notice the interplay of textures – the glossy green leaves and silken blooms.

THE DELICACY OF MAUVE

Mauve, that delicate blend of purple and pink, needs a particularly sensitive touch if you are placing it alongside other, stronger hues. Juxtaposed with bright, eye-catching blooms, its fragile beauty is easily overwhelmed.

In the cottage garden, mauve flowers are often scented – for example, lavender, lilac, phlox, stocks, even the spiky, decorative alliums of the onion family. In winter, pink and mauve hyacinths are the most fragrant of all flowers indoors.

Crocuses and irises are early spring flowers which introduce mauve in small blooms. Place them in small earthenware pots to suggest the way they sprout from the earth so early, taking us by surprise. At Sissinghurst, bearded irises are grown alongside mauve allium clusters and bordered with grey-green sword-shaped leaves – an easy idea to translate indoors in early summer.

In mid-summer, sweet rocket has scented white, pink and mauve flowers to tuck into tricolour bunches, while on a larger scale lilac sprays can tumble from opaque bowls. Florists force lilac to flower out of season, which it does in profusion but with the loss of its heady fragrance. Sweet peas suffer the same fate with market gardeners. The best-scented sweet pea is the old-fashioned mauve *Lathyrus odoratus*, which is small and hooded, with exquisitely subtle colouring.

For bolder arrangements there are mauve hydrangeas, peonies, phlox in the variety 'Fairy's Petticoat', Canterbury bells, hollyhocks and lavender spikes in the deep mauve of 'Hidcote' or the paler, taller 'Munstead'.

Mauve flowers can be emphasized with grey foliage. Felted leaves like those of lamb's ears, silver-sheened leaves of lavender-cotton or senecio or artichoke leaves can all be used to highlight the delicate colour. Or for a nice contrast of texture, place grasses and seed heads among late-summer mauve flowers, such as Michaelmas daisies, to accentuate their meadow-sweet freshness.

In this composition, no single flower is mauve, but the combination of pink and bluebells, whose hues are picked up by the containers and background, coalesces to create an overall mauve effect. White Queen Anne's lace, the greenish-white guelder rose and the grey woolly undersides of viburnum leaves provide colour contrasts. Small flowers like bluebells can easily be overpowered by modern patterned ceramics, but here this effect is avoided by skilful matching of colour tones.

THE SPLENDOUR OF PURPLE

Pure purple, undiluted, is an intense hue, whose strength of colour is best emphasized with dark or pale green, white, blue or pink. In nature and in gardens alike it is seldom pitted against colours of equal vibrancy – although in tropical climes the purple bougainvillea tumbles over sun-splashed walls alongside scarlet and magenta varieties. Such flamboyant combinations need dazzling light and a dash of artlessness to work. In most interiors, the colours would clash.

Yellow, opposite purple on the colour wheel, makes the hue appear more luminous. To gauge the effect, take a simple bunch of miniature pansies (*Viola tricolor*) and set among them sprigs of golden rod, trimmed short: the purple becomes more brilliant, the yellow more pronounced. Now, for a completely different effect, replace the golden rod with a ring of silvery lamb's ears and observe how the purple deepens, becoming markedly bluer.

Large areas of purple in interior decoration have been out of favour since the decades of Art Nouveau. Then, purple was pitted against brilliant blues and greens in the shades of the peacock fantail. Fashionable bouquets at the time included peacock feathers grouped with grasses – an excess introduced by the Viennese painter Hans Makart (1840–84) and known by florists as the "Makart bouquet".

In contemporary interiors, purple is best employed as an accent colour – perhaps distributed in little groups evenly around a room. In early summer, bowls of purple and blue iris are an attractive choice. The tall *Iris sibirica* in the variety 'Keno Gami' lasts well in water. To add informality to regal purples, mix them with white daisies.

Some purple flowers look best massed on their own, not used in mixed bunches. Violets, for example, are best presented in nosegays with a ring of their own deep green leaves: that way they hold their scent and appear just as they would when growing in little clumps in the woodland.

Purple flowers grow in abundance throughout the seasons, so there is a lot to cut. Spring brings *Crocus tomasinianus* and *Iris reticulata*, as well as violets, pansies and anemones. In summer there is deep-purple garden lilac, the heliotrope, Canterbury bells, lupins and delphiniums and late-summer *Buddleia davidii* – known as the butterfly bush.

In this relatively formal arrangement, acanthus spires accompany wild oats, sharp green sedum heads (gathered before they turn pink in late summer) and a silvery grey-green artichoke leaf. The acanthus has a sculptural quality emphasized by its regal colour.

This cheerful composition uses purplish-pink Michaelmas daisies set among dahlia buds, little border carnations and three kinds of bright green leaves – tolmiea, scented geranium and the alchemilla umbrella leaf. As in the other two arrangements, the foliage affects the apparent intensity of the purple.

Mauvish purple tulips are thrown into relief by white lilac, which makes the other hues seem richer, more vivid and more romantic.

THE CHARM OF BLUE

People who say that blue is a cold colour have forgotten the blue of a midsummer sky. That fresh, summery blue is sunny rather than chilling. Forget-me-nots and love-in-a-mist have the same quality of light and warmth.

In the language of interior decoration, many of the blues are named after gemstones. Turquoise, aquamarine, lapis lazuli and sapphire, however, are not found in nature's palette. There you discover the varying blues of cornflowers, periwinkles, gentians, grape hyacinths, bluebells and the blue poppy from the high Himalayas, *Meconopsis betonicifolia*. There is also the range of blues offered by lupins, delphiniums, larkspurs and scabious. Blues are as infinite as the sky in their ability to deepen or lighten according to the petals' bloom. Variations on blue within a single family, such as the delphiniums, can emphasize this dramatic quality. A monochrome blue bunch can move from deepest cobalt to palest azure.

Blue teamed with violet tends toward purple, as you can see in a mixed bunch of anemones. Grey foliage will increase blue's brilliance; or you can sharpen the violet-blue flowers with a dash of lime-green. Low-toned greyish-green foliage highlights true blues, like catmint, borage and cornflowers, but brighter greens struggle a little to assert themselves in such company. A contrast of

This is the traditional way of displaying delphiniums – in towering spires. (Compare the more novel arrangement on the opposite page, far right.) The 'White Lady' lily and the small spreading stars of *Brodiaea* have the effect of purifying the blues; whereas these delphiniums, set among agapanthus, for example, would become thunderously purplish.

blue and yellow, or blue and orange, looks especially vivid when the colours are in equal amounts. Tint or shade either.

Pure blue and red in equal amounts are not restful companions. Red bergamot and blue borage picked from the herb garden and brought indoors for fragrance should have their vividly competing flowers tempered with the silvery grey spikes of another herb, lavender-cotton.

Blue-green or grey leaves can be used to balance blue flowers and create a drift of changing blues, like a seascape – for example, the decorative leaves and bracts of sea holly arranged with agapanthus and spiky blue-grey alliums.

Optically, blue is a receding colour: it appears to move back, away from the viewer. You can exploit this effect by placing blue flowers at the back of a windowsill arrangement, to lead the eye to the garden beyond.

Blue and white flowers can be emphasized by using blue-and-white china as containers. The celebrated *chambre bleue* of Madame de Rambouillet in 17th-century France is one of the classic examples of this colour pairing. White lilies were favoured. This salon made as great an impact on the fashion for bringing cut flowers indoors as did the Dutch floral paintings of the same period.

Blue is both brilliant and pure, one of the more intense colours even when clouded into purples and mauves. Here, the blues of scabious, cornflowers and sprigs of mint in bloom have the luminosity of a mid-summer sky. The simple goblet and low glass bowl were chosen to catch sunlight in this sunny location.

Less is more with this little bouquet of blue delphinium blooms and reed-like grasses. Delphiniums tend to be appreciated entire instead of for the beauty of each individual flower; but this modest arrangement redresses the balance. Snipping off the long graduations of colour from each complete delphinium head has restricted the palette to cobalt blue.

THE FRESHNESS OF GREEN

Green flowers, or flowers with green markings upon them, are more delicate than foliage, and best used without accompanying green leaves. Here, the feathery pinkish green-grey of wild oats makes an ideal combination with astrantia, whose silky pink petals are veined with bold green.

Green is the predominant landscape colour in temperate zones. Green flowers, however, are a novelty, grown for curiosity. Recognize their special impact by using them in isolation, rather than teamed with green's complementary colour red. Or treat them as accent colours in mixed groupings to enliven other hues. The delicacy of green flowers is easily flattened when combined with green foliage. Sometimes, the silvery leaves of senecio or blue-green leaves of rue can highlight a green flower, but mostly green blooms are best isolated from foliage other than their own leaves.

Within a monochrome bunch of green flowers lie many different shades for interest and variety. Flowers tagged 'viridis' are a brilliant apple green – for example, the green bells of false hellebore (*Veratrum viride*). Love-lies-bleeding, commonly red, also includes a brilliant emerald variety, *Amaranthus* 'Viridis'. Some cultivars of the tobacco plant, *Nicotiana*, offer lime-green flowers in mid-summer; zinnia flowers later in the green 'Envy' cultivar. The compact form and ready availability of zinnia from florists make it useful for accent colour in mixed bunches. Similarly, the guelder rose (*Viburnum opulus*) provides a subtle green accent. Some flowers, among them the spurges *Euphorbia robbiae* and *wulfenii*, are yellow-green.

The *Helleborus* genus is a useful source of green flowers throughout the seasons. Some hellebores show silvery greens, like "miniature green water lilies", as Vita Sackville-West observed. There are the great saucer-shaped, lime-green blooms of *H. corsicus*, the lemony-green *H. cyclophyllus*, *H. foetidus*, which produces lemony flowers in spring, and brightest of all, *H. viridis*. Another useful flower is bells of Ireland (*Molucella*), with five-sided, papery bells that cluster on slender green stalks, providing a splash of olive-green – even in winter, as the flower dries well and retains its colour.

In mid summer, when the sunset colours of the garden annuals seem vibrant, the quieter green flowers bring a breath of fresh air to an interior. And in winter, when the landscape is dominated by heavy evergreen foliage, the use of green flowers can be equally lively.

Right:
An arrangement of all-green flowers is as enchanting as it is novel. This low table-piece features the pineapple lily, whose starry flowers cluster upon a dominant waxy green stalk. Green bells of Ireland, a few poppy capsules, some green hydrangea heads and emerald-green *Amaranthus* 'Viridis' contribute different forms and shades within the same colour scheme.

FOLIAGE

Foliage is abundantly available, even at the leanest times of year. Florists' stock in winter ranges from ivy trails to the glossy greens of holly, pieris, osmanthus and escallonia. Plentiful supplies of leaves are also to be found on the shrubs and trees in our own gardens, and you can also clip small quantities of leaves from houseplants to use in floral displays.

The following section eloquently demonstrates the value of using leaves for their singular beauty, not merely as fill-ins for flowers. Their surprising richness of colour, line and pattern, adds visual interest to any arrangement.

Out of doors, the beauty of each leaf is lost in the grand scale; but indoors you notice that leaf sizes, shapes and textures vary as much as their colours. In creative displays the aim is not usually to create a banked mass of green but to show off the individual qualities of different kinds of leaves. Here, the squat hosta leaves are balanced with bridewort (far left), slender phytolacca and bergenia leaves (centre) and, in the right-hand container, *Stephanandra* (which florists call "nut"). A rounded hydrangea bloom brightens the greens of the foliage. The overall effect is an interplay of light, shade and movement.

FIRST LEAVES OF SPRING

Brought indoors, buds will unfurl their colours while winter still has an icy grip on growth. At first the new leaves will hang tremulously on their twigs, like butterflies emerging from chrysalises. To show off these budding branches, place them indoors on a windowsill to catch the light. One or two branches pruned discreetly from garden trees or shrubs will usually be sufficient – or alternatively you can buy branches from a florist. (Practical advice on forcing spring-flowering branches indoors is given on page 186.)

Favourite choices for winter windowsills are the witch hazel for its golden flowers that scent an entire room, the willow *Salix hastata* for its furry grey buds and *Salix daphnoides*, with grey pussy-willow catkins that turn golden.

When branches are the mainstay of an arrangement, it is the quality of the line that counts, not the quantity.

The bare stems in contrast to the early buds make an emphatic statement. Set them in glass containers so that the lines are uninterrupted. Simplicity is best.

The charm of the first leaves of spring lies partly in their transience – the colour changes they undergo before reaching mid-summer uniformity. On the beech *Fagus sylvatica* 'Riversii' and the flowering cherry, translucent pinks turn to solid purple. The first red leaves of pieris pass through gold to green. Similarly, the golden leaves of maple are sober green by mid-summer. *Astilbe x arendsii* can be picked in spring for its feathery pinkish-purple leaves, which become green when the flowers appear. The plantain lily *Hosta fortunei* 'Albopicta' is initially striped lime-green with emerald, and later turns primrose and dark green. *Philadelphus coronarius* 'Aureus' has fresh yellow leaves that deepen to green.

Left: **In a restrained indoor display, a mixture of green and copper beech has a lightness and delicacy never observed when the leaves are massed together in a clipped suburban hedge. Arum lilies, azalea buds and a few sprigs of *Euphorbia wulfenii* are in the tallest vase, while white lilac and guelder rose anchor the composition at the front. The compact form of these smaller foreground elements prevents the backdrop of leaves from appearing too straggly.**

A tall glass cylinder holds shapely branches of whitebeam. Rather than hammer the cut edges at the base to assist the water intake to the leaves, I slit the woody stems at intervals up to two inches above the cut. Whitebeam lasts well in water.

Green foliage in flower arrangements brings an interior closer to nature. The colour also brings you tranquillity. It is a physiological fact, not just popular fancy, that of all hues green is most restful to look at, requiring no focusing adjustments.

Mid-way between blue and yellow on the spectrum, the green of leaves may be tinged either way. Leaves on old tapestries and fabrics are often blue, because a composite of blue and yellow dyes was used to achieve the original greens, and with time the yellows have faded. To evoke the richness of tapestries at home, there are numerous plants whose leaves supply the necessary shades – for example, eucalyptus, olive, rue 'Jackman's Blue' and sage. Botanists call these blue-greens "glaucous". Glaucous leaves make adjacent colours seem more brilliant by contrast. Purer greens tend to make neighbouring blooms look redder, but by including glaucous leaves instead you can avoid this effect.

Imitate nature by mixing shades of green for a pleasingly variegated effect. Mix blue-green species with lime-green ferns or the yellow-green flowers of the tobacco plant. Use dark-green rose foliage – for example, *Rosa rubrifolia* (*glauca*), the woolly little grey-green leaves of helichrysum or glossy evergreens to ring the changes on shade or texture.

Few monochrome schemes work as well as the peaceful greens. Inspiration for different greens emphasized by variations of line and shape comes from the all-green Italian Renaissance garden. Here we find the dark-green exclamation mark of the cypress rising above ranks of paler box, or rounded grey-green olive leaves in parentheses of arching wisteria. You can imitate this inventiveness on a domestic scale, replacing Italianate formalism with a more natural, instinctive approach. For arrangements that suggest the wilderness beyond our windows, snip bunches of green from hedgerows. In particular, look for leafy cowparsley, the leathery little galax ruff and trails of wandering ivy. Look too for lady's mantle, whose yellow-green umbrella-shaped leaf is designed to hold a drop of water in its central hub.

Flowering shrubs are all too often cut for the flowers rather than the leaves. Here, however, the foliage, in many shades of green, predominates. The pink Canterbury bells and kolkwitzia and pink roses were chosen to emphasize the pale pink flowers on the great arching stems of *Deutzia*, which gives outline to the single branch of dogwood (*Cornus alba* 'Elegantissima'). Splashed with gold, the dogwood's leaves make a sunny central focus for the bouquet, accentuated by the gold-green dill heads in the foreground. To complete the arrangement, mock orange (too often stripped of its pretty oval leaves so that the scented flower heads get more water), provides well-formed leafy branches and fine red stems.

Green is seldom used alone – which is a pity, because an all-green arrangement can look pleasing. This green sedum with its waxy, toothed leaves and umbels of grey-green flowers has a sculptural quality. Several hosta leaves curl protectively over the sedum, their golden-green veinings presenting a finely tuned contrast. The dramatic black and white spatter-glaze vase heightens the theatrical effect.

VARIATIONS AND VARIEGATIONS

Leaves may be veined, stippled, scumbled, shaded, dappled, gilded or marbled, in a wide range of colours and textures. Botanists refer to these remarkable patternings as "blotches and marks", as though they were an affliction. But for flower designers, such markings offer a wealth of aesthetic effects.

Variegated leaves should be massed in big bunches, rather than set in snippets among flowers. Choose a location with plenty of light to show off the markings, and be sure to select a sympathetic setting: the special patterned paint effects that are favoured in modern interiors make an excellent background.

Combine different species whose characteristics complement each other in colour or texture. For example, you could mix the green-and-gold leaves of *Elaeagnus pungens* 'Maculata' with Persian ivy (*Hedera colchica* 'Dentata Variegata), also in green and gold – and

perhaps tuck in some variegated mint for a change of texture. Gold splashes on leaves convincingly evoke the play of sunlight.

Snippings from house plants are a useful source of dappled foliage – such as red-and-green-marbled caladium leaves or the bristly metallic sheen on plum-and-green *Begonia rex*. The leaves of many house plants root in water; begonia, ivy, coleus, busy-lizzie and geranium, for example, will multiply quickly from leaf cuttings.

Some leaves are valued for their eye-catching shapes or textures as much as for their colouring. Spiny branches of barberry, deeply-cut elder leaves or finely-divided, downy-leaved artemisia are just three examples out of many. Do not neglect, either, the unusual possibilities offered by ornamental vegetables, notably cabbage and kale, as used in the arrangement illustrated in the centre picture here.

Below left: **This foliage trio in an unstoppered inkwell would be suitable for a desktop. The sculptural emerald-edged green leaves are *Hosta fortunei* 'Albopicta', known as the plantain lily. As summer advances, the green band darkens and the bright yellow bleaches to primrose. Bringing out the golden aura of the hosta with a perfect colour contrast is plum-veined *Caladium bicolor*, a flamboyant leaf from South America. A few fresh green tolmiea leaves complete this leaf corsage.**

Below: **All the foliage colours – blues, greens, greys and plums – are combined here. Eucalyptus leaves arch in graceful sprays from the tallest vase, with fronds of artemisia and fresh green mint, allowed to flower in a spire of mauve. Height is provided by pretty white *Eustoma* blooms. The mauve is echoed in the foreground with ornamental cabbage, its purple highlighted by eye-catching white *Helichrysum* in the mug.**

Knotweed (*Polygonum*) is used here in a richly ornamented spherical vase with a wide mouth to support the tumbling sprays. A rampant and vigorous climber, knotweed is cut in autumn for its white flowers. Like all climbers, it needs to be lavishly cut to bunch in masses. The giant leaves in the arrangement are gunnera.

FERNS AND GRASSES

Free growth and elegant outlines distinguish ferns and grasses, yet flower arrangers have been slow to make best use of these qualities. Grasses indoors are mostly dried, sometimes sprayed gold or silver, to add to arid, crackly, dried bouquets that gather dust in many a forlorn setting. Avoid such sorry exhibits: instead, use fresh grasses, perhaps teamed with fresh-cut flowers.

Ornamental grasses, on long stems, are valued for their delicacy and grace. Quaking grass, responsive to the slightest breeze, and arching blue oats grass, are particularly attractive. A favourite in turn-of-the-century settings is pampas grass, which grows white feathery panicles: these look best against dark backgrounds.

Ferns are also of great value for indoor displays. Use a tub of ferns as a full-stop to a line-up of flower vases, or stand a big tub at floor level so that a curving frond frames a display of blooms. Alternatively, trim delicate fronds to tuck like a lacy ruff around a container rim.

Before the days of central heating, it was necessary to grow ferns in conservatories, but in today's centrally heated rooms they are quite happy, provided that you give enough moisture. The bathroom offers an ideal environment for the ubiquitous black-stemmed maidenhair ferns, as well as ferns with spear-shaped leaves, such as the bird's nest fern (*Asplenium nidus*).

Bamboos, like ferns, bring a delicate outline to arrangements. Many types are invasive and can be freely cut to bring indoors from the garden.

Above left: **Grasses picked from a wild garden offer variegations and contrasting textures that draw the eye inward, to focus on details of the display.**

Above: **Viewed against a muted abstract watercolour by William Tillyer, these bamboo fronds stand out with graphic immediacy. The bamboo has been placed so that the oblique lines of the leaves fall in the same direction as the shafted brush strokes of the painting.**

Left: **A few fronds of grasses placed in a bold container against a plain dark background can make an effective display, which draws our attention to the ripening seeds. Here, the slender delicacy of the tall grasses is in contrast with the hydrangea head in a clear glass bowl.**

Below: **Frosted glass with a patterned sandblasted finish is here juxtaposed with the tracery of maidenhair fern. The opaque glass silhouettes the fern's slender stalks, throwing more emphasis on the delicacy of the fronds.**

SHADES OF GREY

Grey foliage is mostly metallic and burnished in appearance – with a touch of silver, lead, pewter or steel, or sometimes ash. Unlike green leaves, shades of grey look sombre in monochrome. However, they are a good foil for colour, making the hues of neighbouring blooms and of the container seem more brilliant by contrast. This treatment is especially effective with pale flowers, such as the Christmas rose. Daisies, chrysanthemums and zinnia (whose green leaves wilt fast in water) are also improved by the addition of silvery foliage, which makes a good counterpoint to their open-faced brightness. Grey also brings out the acid sharpness of lime-green flowers such as hellebores or euphorbia.

The white garden at Sissinghurst is a fruitful source of inspiration. Here, there is an underplanting of grey lavender-cotton, with senecio, camomile, sea ragwort and blue-grey *Hosta sieboldiana*. Among all this silvery foliage, the white and cream flowers look exquisite. On a smaller scale indoors, that combination of grey and white works just as well. With lavender-cotton, senecio and furry grey lambs' ears you can mix creamy peonies and white hybrid roses (such as 'Pascali'), evening primroses and white irises outlined with gold.

Some grey-leaved plants have a sculptural appearance that works well in a modern interior. Examples of these living works of art are the sea holly, artichoke and Scotch thistle. Set at floor level in big containers, these tall plants can stand alone, dignified and regal. Some flowering plants, such as lavender and carnation, have a much smaller, more uniform grey leaf which will survive the winter.

The light in which you view grey foliage is important. In a dark corner, or at twilight, it will take on a mysterious mauve glow. But in midday sun, grey leaves will have a steely glint.

Grey makes neighbouring colours more intense. *Crocosmia* is lightened by contrast with grey senecio. Next to the orange, the grey leaves become distinctly silvery in tone. Replace the orange flowers with scarlet salvia and the grey would be suffused with green; next to violet, it would move toward yellow.

This arrangement shows subtle contrasts within the blue-grey spectrum. Eucalyptus, rue 'Jackman's Blue' and the mauve sea holly are deepened with the addition of artemisia's feathery foliage and lime-green *Euphorbia wulfenii*. None of the foliage blues have the brilliance of blue flowers, but a smoky subtlety with a hint of slate.

CONTAINERS

Containers transform flowers. They affect the colour and the texture of the bloom, as well as that indefinable quality, mood. Designing with flowers is the alliance between container and flower. Change the container and you have a different design.

The following section shows how Tricia Guild brings verve and imagination to her use of containers – not only ceramic and glass bowls and vases but also less orthodox flower holders such as baskets, teapots, old medicine bottles, household pots and even fish tanks. Collecting containers has the magical ability to turn itself into a commitment. There are no limits to the possibilities: a true scavenger can turn anything to use.

An idiosyncratic collection of containers such as this one – with zigzags, swirls, dashes and crosses – needs simple but strong flowers to compete. By trimming short the stems, attention is focused on the jugs, with their jolts of fresh coral *hippeastrum* amaryllis lily. Longer stems would have carried that glowing colour too far from the china to make an impact. The use of empty containers alongside flower-filled ones is an effective strategy.

GLASS

Imagine roses in dusky pink and apricot spilling out of a simple cream jug. The juxtaposition of the plain ceramic holder and the glowing, velvety blooms might have come from a Vuillard painting. But trim the stems of the same roses and set the bunch in a cut-glass goblet on a polished wooden table and the effect is quite different. The flowers take on the clarity of the glass, as the contrast between the colours is highlighted and sharpened by the dark green stems showing through it.

The best way to avoid an artificial arrangement is to learn to appreciate the natural form of the flowers you use. Glass containers, which will hide nothing, make the use of props out of the question. No crumpled wire netting, spiked mat or water-absorbent foam to regiment flowers can be hidden in glass. Instead, you have to arrange the flowers according to the manner in which they grow – whether they trail and bend like nasturtiums or clematis or grow tall and rigid like hyacinths or iris. Each presentation will be determined by the character of the particular flowers used.

Above: **Four little glass jars support fresh nosegays of flowers in all the clear yellows and lime-greens of early spring: narcissus, guelder rose, Queen Anne's lace, *Helleborus foetidus* and *Euphorbia robbiae*.**

Right: **Big glass containers do not always have to be crowded with flowers. Try displaying just a half-dozen or so, varying the heights and singling out the colours. In this display, 'Carte Blanche' roses have** been trimmed to line the neck of a tall, wide container with a frilled edge of white, alongside spotted pulmonaria leaves. Three slender pink stocks rise from the arrangement.

The first step to acquiring a natural touch in flower arranging is to put a simple bunch of flowers into a simple glass vase. This is where the art of composition begins.

There are many specially designed glass cubes, cylinders and bowls available. A cube or cylinder with a diameter of seven or eight inches is particularly useful, and holds a bouquet of up to three dozen flowers. But use your imagination – a fishtank or a goldfish bowl from a pet shop could be perfect.

Whatever the container, its neck must be the right width to support the bunch: too wide and the flowers will flop, too narrow and they lose their natural grace. The depth must be sufficient too, though the length of the stems can be trimmed to fit. The mouth of the container should be at least half the diameter of the bunch itself, so that the stems are not squeezed together, but hold each other in place with room to move and sway a little. Tulips, for example, continue to grow in water, and need room to twist and bend. All the stems, of course, must reach the water.

Because glass containers show everything, you must strip away any leaves below the water line, leaving only a few for decoration. Remember to split woody stems two inches from the base to help water intake: you could crush them for the same effect, but this would look unsightly. Eliminate any broken or misshapen stems. Then take the bunch in your hand and cut all the stems right across, to suit the depth of the glass. Let them fall easily from your hand into the container and the movement of the flowers will create a natural design.

For massed sprays, perhaps the tumbling garden lilac or bright clusters of rhododendrons, a wider-necked glass container will be needed. Shrubby blossoms, massed together, need their foliage to separate the blooms, but remove some of the leaves on the sprays to assist the water intake.

If heavy sprays topple to the sides of the bowl, leave them there, and fill in the middle of the arrangement with more foliage – sprigs of slender-stemmed, upright green spurge or greeny-yellow hellebore flowers.

Glass containers discourage the use of artificial aids to marshal flowers. I used a clear glass cube here, letting natural form dictate the arrangement. The fleshy stalks of 'Stargazer' lily form a lattice with woody white lilac and oak below water level. Tucked loosely into the trellis are sprigs of golden-green *Euphorbia polychroma* and, in the background, the green *Euphorbia robbiae*. With such wide-mouthed containers you often need to trim stalks to prevent flowers from toppling.

GLASS

It often helps to criss-cross the stems so that they form a light webbing which gives support to slender-stemmed flowers. In a glass container this latticed appearance becomes an attractive part of the composition. The effect will be spoiled, though, if the water is allowed to become stale and green. Glass containers will remind you to add fresh water daily.

Finally, make use of single-stem vases in clear glass. Intended for buds, they are perfect for open blooms or tiny posies, which can be distributed round the house or clustered together to make a single table-top display.

A pincushion of mixed solid colours packed into the glass basket at the right of this table would have spoiled its delicate lines. More attractive is this use of a free, informal bunch of hedgerow pickings framed by the curving glass handle: there is Queen Anne's lace, a single creamy spray of sweet peas and two dock leaves. In the taller goblet, blue love-in-a-mist, borage and cornflowers team with Queen Anne's lace.

Right: Of course, glass containers for flowers need not be transparent. The left-hand container here is an opalescent Lalique glass bowl, which provides a soft base for the delicate tracery of meadow rue (*Thalictrum*). A figurine and tiny rabbit in an echoing Art Nouveau style turn the arrangement into a still life. In the clear container on the right, country garden sweet peas with a single spray of meadow rue harmonize well.

The colour, shape and texture of ceramic containers make a bolder contribution to an arrangement than translucent glass. Because ceramics are opaque they are perfect for woody plants whose stems have been well crushed at the base to enable them to take in more water. Ceramic vases in simple shapes and larger sizes are ideal for the bigger branches and sprays.

Historically, ceramic containers were planned as an aspect of interior design, and seldom changed. The *tulipières* of the 17th century were pottery containers, each with four spouts, grouped together in pyramids. 18th-century spout vases, joined together in a fan shape, were based on the earlier slender-necked flasks for single blooms which came from China. Josiah Wedgwood made ceramic containers with perforated lids for flower stalks. Nowadays, any suitable vessel can be used, whether it was originally intended to hold flowers or not.

Flowers look especially fresh against the earthy colour of terracotta, as shown by this arrangement of *Alchemilla mollis* and *Brodiaea*, mixed with a little purplish-white *Astrantia* and accompanied by the house plant *Helxine soleirolii* in the garden pot at the right of the picture.

Ceramic containers in sky blue and soft green intensify the blue of larkspur and delphinium, and sharpen the green hellebore and beech. A pink peony against the glossy leafed choisya is unexpectedly bold. Brighter containers make colour contrasts more vivid.

Plain vases are, perhaps, the easiest to fill with flowers. The muted plains will complement the widest range of flowers and be at home in most colour schemes. Pale shades of wicker, alabaster or marble, and earthenware with glazes in celadon green, buff, grey or white, will suit almost any background and grace any flower. Plain, vibrantly coloured vases are useful for colour accents.

A room's distinctive character dictates the choice of container. Choose the right place for the flowers and then select the container. Fine porcelain would be too grand for sheaves of corn and poppies set on the kitchen windowsill, while an earthenware jug filled with scented stocks would be less pleasing placed in a formal chintz drawing room than the same flowers in a porcelain bowl.

An element of surprise works well. For example, begonia leaves, or coleus with its ornate markings, can stand in ceramic pots among a group of cut flowers in a vase.

PATTERNED CERAMICS

Left: **On these vases, lines of pink dots create a colour echo with the pink-spotted markings of the 'Rubrum' lily and pinkish buds of *L. regale*. Clusters of pink larkspur and catmint give height to the arrangement to balance the proportions of the identical vases; they also introduce vertical pink bands that echo the decorations on the ceramics. (The vases were made by Janice Tchalenko.)**

Below: **Although shaped like a common or garden earthenware pot, this ceramic holder has more individuality, with its painted daubs of white and grey. In such a jolly pot, you need cheerful plants: open-faced gerbera daisies in pinks, oranges and scarlet, together with an impromptu bunch of green bells of Ireland and some purple-berried St John's wort.**

Right: **The solid grey of these pots, with their black patterning, could flatten all but the most distinctively coloured flowers. The coral trumpets of amaryllis are a good choice, as they are strong enough not to be overwhelmed by the graphic lines of these modern ceramics. White lilac in bud and whitebeam leaves were added to reduce the scale and contribute a touch of delicacy. The grey of the tall jug deepens the coral petals.**

Today, photographs of fashionable interiors seldom show patterned vases. Glass or plain ceramics are less demanding and thus more commonplace. Yet a patterned vase, well shaped for flowers and set against the right background, contributes more to the decoration of a room than a plain one. The right widemouthed patterned ceramic container, for example, can be perfect for a country garden mix of peonies, ranunculus, hellebore, white guelder rose and a tangle of leaves.

Patterned ceramics come from a long tradition. Boldly patterned early Greek and Roman vases and Etruscan *bas-relief* urns were the models which provided inspiration for the neoclassical period, when vases were emblazoned with medallions and ornamented with swags, bows and satyr masks.

Art Nouveau saw the flowering of an ornate style in painted lustre-ware vases decorated in subtle colours with sword-like leaves, lilies and even mushrooms. Then Art Deco vases were boldly painted with flowers and leaves, outlined in black.

Modern ceramics with their speckled or spattered glazes and distinctive shapes will often complement traditional interiors as well as contemporary rooms.

BLUE-AND-WHITE

The blue-and-white willow pattern of ancient China tells the story of the plight of the Mandarin's daughter, Koong See: imprisoned by her father, she escapes in the spring, when the fruit trees are in bud, across a bridge to meet her lover, Chang. These two identical vases tell the legend in different aspects, and are appropriately filled with different flowers – spires of blue delphiniums and greenish-yellow *Alchemilla mollis.* The accompanying ginger jars continue the colour scheme, but the smaller one (with cornflowers) attractively reverses the colours, with a blue ground instead of white.

Blue-and-white china looks good, not only with food, but also with many flowers. If you collect blue-and-white, you will probably be drawn to flowers of a certain colour range. Flowers in all the shades of blue – anemones in winter, iris, grape hyacinths, bluebells and crocuses in spring, delphiniums, larkspur, cornflowers and agapanthus in summer – suit a range of blue-and-white china ware in a combination of shapes and patterns. Too often associated exclusively with kitchens, blue-and-white looks marvellous in any interior. Massed bunches of roses set in a blue-and-white pitcher are at home anywhere – country cottage, elegant period house or starkly modern apartment.

Blue-and-white, reminiscent of the Aegean sea and its white-washed buildings or sunny summer skies with white clouds, is fresh but never cold. Lime-green flowers and dark green leaves, white and gold, and all the pinks and reds, look just as good in this combination as do blues and purples.

Big blue and white ginger jars make ideal floor-standing holders for branches and sprays which change with the months: the graceful arching winter jasmine, red-flowering quince, golden broom, dogwood stems, yellow maple, bronzed beech leaves or hawthorn berries.

Below: **Modern ceramist Janice Tchalenko has created a modern variation of the blue-and-white theme, using a carefree combination of blue lines interlacing each other, dotted here and there with olive green. With fresh flowers in the vases, the greenish dots become more prominent, strengthened by the yellowish green of** *Alchemilla mollis*. **Wild pink yarrow links the lemony greens, while a bowl of soft, golden potpourri petals serves as a full stop to the display, returning to the pattern after an interval of pure white.**

Left: **An apricot ruff anchors the base of this patterned pot: above it, the dappled blues and white of a swirling midsummer sky. The flowers repeat that horizon line of distant trees against the sky, with blue and white delphiniums and young beech leaves rising from dark green Solomon's seal, whose small white bells are shaded beneath the leaves. These cool drifts of blue, white and green have a spacious outdoor feel about them.**

The gleam of metal makes a subdued base for flowers, to suit a whole range of settings. A polished dining table set with porcelain, cut glass and silver in a room with swagged and bowed drapes might call for a 19th-century silver épergne as a grand flower-holding centrepiece. At the other end of the scale, a simple copper bowl, a jam jar of water hidden inside it, reflects the undisciplined nasturtiums spilling over the rim; or an old pewter mug adds a burnished gleam to match the autumn maturity of scarlet rose hips and yellow maple leaves.

The colour of metal affects the tones of the flowers. Warm purples and pinks are cooled by silver, and strong blues subdued. A silver bowl can make white roses look a little grand and austere for a formal room, or the pale lavenders, pinks, dark crimson and creams of garden sweet peas look coolly summery.

Bronze and copper give a warmer glint. A bronze bowl with embossed decorative birds or vines is opulent and fruity. A bronze or copper tray gives a pleasing firelight gleam to snowberries and late pink floribunda roses laid upon its surface.

Even a tin pail or galvanized metal watering can makes a sturdy but charming container, given a coat of paint. These are heirs to the bargeboat tradition of tinware trays, water jugs, pails and mugs, which were often painted by the ceramic painters to whom the canal boats ferried clay. This traditional tinware, naively decorated with bright motifs, can still be found today, and used as containers for simple daisies, poppies, grasses and cornflowers.

Far left: **A dark cast-iron bowl suggests strength and resilience, and needs a delicate combination of flowers in fresh-looking colours to contest that impression. Here, flat-top hydrangeas in pink, blue and white, together with *Stephanandra* leaves, offer a charming antidote to the severity of matt black. In close-up** (near left), **the iron container reveals a surprising delicacy, with delightful embellishments of birds and irises upon its curving side. The pinks and blues of the hydrangeas, spilling from the bowl, offer a protective and colourful bower around this ornamentation.**

Above: **In this unusual arrangement, an old galvanized cannister is placed on an unorthodox but thoroughly compatible base – a chromium wire shelf, which provides a geometric background to contrast with the spider dahlia. Teamed with the dahlia are a few sprigs of *Stephanandra* leaves and purpling *Hypericum* berries.**

A basket makes a charmingly informal flower container. In this one the water is held in a thick stiff plastic bag, loosely bound with twine around the flower stems, and hidden by the blooms. The flowers appropriately evoke the countryside – annual mauve and blue scabious, the leaves of hops, *Hypericum* seed heads and variegated ivy. This display would make a welcoming feature for a hall table.

Left: **An effective way to use a wicker basket is to fill it with a profusion of long flower heads arranged so that they tumble out in arching spires at all four points of the compass. Here there is eucalyptus, mimosa, sea holly, *Protea*, and flowering mint for its fragrance. It is fun to combine a big arrangement with a small one, the difference in scale making the larger one seem more full of flowers than it really is. This is the idea of the little jar at the left, which holds a few cornflowers, white anemones and mimosa.**

Below: **Bare boards make an unaffected background for a little basket, filled with a fresh bunch of scented mock orange, *Alchemilla mollis*, fennel and a deep blue cornflower, centrally placed to draw the attention.**

From a practical point of view, containers must be able to nourish the cut plants as well as give them physical support. In other words, they have to hold water. But bear in mind that you can hold the water in an invisible lining, placed inside the outer, visible container. Plastic tubs, freezer boxes, baking dishes and pans, old jam-jars – all can be recruited to be placed inside a container that is not in itself watertight. Almost any container can be made to work if it is right for the flowers and the room – wicker baskets included.

A woven basket, set in a place where it will not be moved, can be filled with country flowers, their stems in a stiff plastic bag half-filled with water and tied up loosely round the bunch with twine.

A shallow basket, used to briefly carry cut flowers from the garden, can provide an unexpected contrast indoors with a display of potted plants from the garden or greenhouse. Little primulas and crocuses can be lined up inside, their terracotta pots hidden by the woven sides. Or a wicker tray, painted white, can hold a shallow bedding tray full of plants in flower – the powderpuff blue of ageratum or a miniature field of pansies will create a pool of colour in a room. The plants themselves can later be planted out in the garden or a window box, where they will have another lease of life.

UNUSUAL CONTAINERS

Household objects, or even objects found on junk stalls or in the garden shed, can be a fruitful source of containers for flower arranging. All you need is an eye for the unexpected, and almost anything can be transformed and turned to good use. If the container itself is not watertight, conceal inside it a vessel that is. If instability is a problem, use pieces of adhesive gum to help maintain the balance.

Shape and size are the main criteria for suitability. Combine small holders in groups to emphasize their special qualities. Empty scent bottles, earthenware mustard jars, old medicine bottles (especially those in blue glass) should be saved. Kitchen breadcrocks, lidless casseroles, soup tureens, jelly moulds, pewter mugs, even teapots and cups, could be ideal for particular arrangements.

A keen eye will suggest endless ideas. Perceive an object not for what it is but for what it might become. A tall spaghetti jar without its stopper can hold long white marguerite daisies, fresh and simple. Even a paint-splashed pail can become a giant tumbler for huge cabbage roses in splashy colours.

Far right: **Low bowls, like small pools, invite our leisurely gaze. In the left-hand bowl here, the blue gentian matches the blue of the container. In the widest bowl, two pink zinnias are afloat; and in the foreground are pale pink anemones, sparsely arranged to show the container markings.**

Right: **In this close-up, you can see how the pattern on the ceramic bowls is matched by the intensity of colour in the fresh blooms.**

Above: **An overhead view of a simple three-part table arrangement. The blue gentians contrast effectively with the pink azalea.**

Right: **Colourful teapots and coffee pots are commonplace items in kitchens, but few people think of filling them with flowers. This is a good way to create a bold colour contrast. Here, I used scabious, zinnia, gentian and a few leaves of** *Stephanandra*. **The lids placed to the side of the tea pots make casual pools of colour upon the tabletop.**

GROUPING CONTAINERS

Sometimes each flower needs its own vase. Exquisite blooms such as an out-of-season rose, a single lily or a tropical orchid are the first to come to mind, but more commonplace flowers set alone can also look effective – especially when you display them in grouped containers. Five or seven daffodils, trimmed to flower head height and set in a cluster of bud vases upon a marbled fireplace, may be more inspiring than several times that number massed together in a jug.

The art of grouping grows naturally from an appreciation of plants and their habits. With a generous bouquet, it is often better to divide the bunch and put the overflow in a separate container rather than to stuff the whole bouquet into something too narrow: and if you do this, you have already created a grouped arrangement.

Display today is quite a different art from that of the 18th century, when lidded pots, matched up in size and height to the flowers, were set neatly in rows on hearths and mantelshelves, or the 19th century, when neo-classical vases stood proudly in pairs. The 20th century takes a very different approach and

When grouping a "chorus line" of flower containers, you should make the most of different shapes and sizes, while preserving a degree of continuity in the flowers or the container colours. In this group the centrepiece – centre-stage, as it were – is the tallest glass cube, holding the celebratory 'Champagne' roses, a caladium leaf, lilac in bud, and stocks. The same flowers with the addition of *Euphorbia*, are scattered among the other four jars and cubes, tying their differences together in a harmonious ensemble.

casually groups vases to vary height and dimensions.

Glass vases like a hybrid between a small jam jar and a flask are ideal for groups. Their necks are just wide enough to take a small nosegay or a large single flower. The separate vases can be lined up, the flowers trimmed to different heights, to give a flowing line; or they can be clustered closely, the blossoms touching in a single splash of colour.

In spring, small glass vases may be filled with little flowers gathered into bouquets: snowdrops, crocuses, scilla, daffodils, grape hyacinths, primroses, violets. In summer, a lily trumpet, tawny and flecked or banded with gold, may be placed alongside a spray of feathery grass. Delphinium heads or single hollyhock blooms separated from the spire and set singly in bud vases will attract individual attention to their singular beauty instead of being viewed together. Three or four small vases of flowers on a desk and several more placed in a room on occa-sional tables or on windowsills will ensure that each flower is appreciated for itself rather than contributing to a mass effect.

Grouping at eye-level provides an opportunity to observe the form and texture of each flower, rather in the manner of the beds, troughs or urns used by gardeners to display rare species and alpine plants.

Several glass containers of different sizes may be grouped together to form a table-top still life. A mixture of tall cylinders may hold spring leaves in contrasting colours and textures, with smaller glasses holding buds clustered beneath them. This sort of grouping is an exercise in balance and proportion.

For a table setting, little peat pots make splendid impromptu holders for single corms or tubers of spring flowers lined up along a fine table-cloth, beside crystal and silver table-ware. The dark peat creates an earthy contrast to the rest of the table setting, and each flower can be appreciated.

In this grouping, patterned ceramics in blue and white are combined with clear glass. Continuity is provided by the oblique profile, rising to the right. Within this carefully graduated line-up there is a rich mix of flowers: pink and blue cornflowers in the mug, then purple *Brodiaea* in the glass carafe, love-in-a-mist in the shapely foreground flask, a mixture of *Brodiaea* with a few scabious and several cornflower buds in the fourth container, and pink cornflowers in the right-hand, tallest vase. Observe how the flower colour shifts from pink and intensely blue, then dapples into mauvish pink, and back into undiluted pink with the cornflowers.

THE ART OF COMPOSITION

Even a single flower in a glass flask on the windowsill is a composition. Add further flasks with foliage or other blooms, and the effect becomes more complex. At its most elaborate, a flower arrangement consists of various elements in a controlled relationship with each other – colour, form, line, texture, pattern, proportion, all working together to achieve a harmonious display.

Whichever approach you take, you must rely on your instincts, standing back at intervals to judge the impact and making adjustments accordingly. There are no rules – except that you must always strive to achieve a natural effect that does justice to the individual qualities of the flowers. The following section of the book shows the rewards of this natural approach.

A grouped composition relies on counterpoints between the flowers and foliage in different containers and between the containers themselves. Notice here how the cornflowers and leaning sprig of alkanet (centre) pick up the principal container colour, while the feathery grasses provide endstops, unifying the different containers. The shrub roses and white hydrangea panicle supply colour accents. The overall profile is a graceful double curve, concluding in the rounded form of the grasses at the right.

KEEPING IT SIMPLE

Just one or two flowers on their own in a vase can be stunning in their simplicity. Find the right location to complement the colour and texture, add a few props, and the arrangement becomes a living still life. This is a good approach to take with flowers that do not last well in water: fast-fading flowers are not suited to complex mixed bunches, because you too quickly have to renew the whole assembly.

By showing flowers in isolation, you focus attention on them, so you should always choose perfect blooms. The more lavishly proportioned species are preferable. However exquisite, a single grape hyacinth on its own in a bud vase looks as forlorn as a single bluebell in a wood; yet a lone Dutch hyacinth is splendidly decorative, and will fill a whole room with fragrance.

Showing off blooms in small numbers lessens their colour impact – a useful ploy when you want to tone down bold colours. A large uniform bunch of yellow marigolds, for example, could overpower a pastel pink room, yet two or three blooms reflected in a gilded mirror would provide a welcome jolt of sunny colour. Similarly, in a blue and white room a mass of purple delphiniums would be taxing to the eye, whereas a solitary spire introduces a useful vertical accent.

Narrow-necked containers or flasks are ideal for single or paired flowers; if you wish, you can add a ruff of leaves so that the flower head on its long stalk appears to push up through undergrowth. However, an unaccompanied bloom can be bold enough to warrant a more theatrical treatment, in a container larger than the flower head. For example, you might place a single scarlet parrot tulip in a large decorative bowl, with only the frilled edges of the petals showing above the rim; place this on a low table to reveal the eye-catching

pool of glowing red inside the bowl. Another display for a low table might be a peony head afloat in a shallow bowl, its pink petals edged with a decorative collar of grey-green artichoke leaves.

Each season brings a new crop of flowers for single display. In spring there is the Dutch iris, the hyacinth and the tulip; in early summer the peony, rose, lilies and the carnation, which has the formality of a buttonhole when used on its own. Later in the summer come the guelder rose, the geranium, and more lilies. Suitable winter blooms include the

camellia, as well as the water lily for floating in a shallow container as a table centrepiece.

Branches, buds, leaves and berries also merit simple treatment. For example, you could lay golden and red berries in patterns of glowing colour upon a wooden board, or cupped in a shallow wooden or pewter bowl. Choose a branch for its elegant shape and place it in a heavy ceramic jug on a window-ledge; shown off in this way, the leaves of whitebeam, mountain ash or beech will acquire a beautiful translucence as the sunlight catches them.

These ingredients are very simple – a shallow dish and a group of gerbera daisy heads in pink and red laid across a spray of St Johns wort. Seemingly casual, the arrangement is in fact artfully composed, forming a bold squiggle of colour across the neutral grey background.

Left: **House plants growing in pots can be a useful addition to fresh cut flowers. On the left of this grouping, mossy green** *Helxine* **contributes dense mounds of green to balance with tall, spindly fennel stalks, stripped of their leaves. The white** *Lilium longiflorum* **flowers in the central container have been trimmed to curve gracefully like swans' necks. The overall effect evokes a watery landscape – tall reeds, mossy banks, and white flowers at water level. Two guelder roses among** *Alchemilla mollis* **complete the pastoral picture.**

It can be effective to mix just two or three flowers with clusters of tiny blooms, for a strong contrast of scale. These four gerbera daisies and a few green azalea stems stripped of their fluttery leaves tower over lime-green *Euphorbia wulfenii* **and lilac. The minimalist arrangement in the right-hand vase is a deliberate touch of understatement.**

The florist delivers a bouquet. Your sense of anticipation grows as you unfurl the crackly cellophane and plan how best to display the bunch in your room. Provided that you proceed slowly and carefully, there are few better opportunities for introducing colour and life into an interior.

To condition the flowers you must place them neck-high in water for a long soak while you select the most suitable location and container. Colour is the primary consideration. Hold the flowers, loosely bunched, against the receptacle that you have chosen and assess the colour combination. Let your eyes guide you in their immediate response, and discard any discordant colours. For example, a yellow pompon chrysanthemum tucked into a bunch of pastel pink roses would have to be removed and used separately in another grouping: neither the colours nor the textures are complementary.

Once you are happy with the coupling of flowers and container, double-check whether the ensemble works well against your chosen background. If so, you are now ready to build up the composition. Leave the flowers soaking in deep water while you create the framework with leaves, beginning at the outer corners and working toward the central point. Consider the heights carefully, trimming the branches with scissors as you position them. Unless you want a deliberately tight bunch, it helps loosely to interlace the branches and thicker stems to provide a casual lattice within the container; this will support the finer-stemmed flowers.

Keep in mind an imaginary outline as you place the foliage. Move about the branches freely to obtain the desired profile: you can create a compact, rounded outline, a vertical one, a range of peaks and valleys, or horizontal, spreading shapes.

Stand back at this stage to observe the effect. Now you have the outline, you can begin to add brush strokes of colour, like a painter filling in a canvas. Unlike an artist, however, you need not fill in every space. Knowing where to stop is as important to the flower designer as knowing where to begin. As the arrangement opposite tellingly shows, restraint can be a virtue. Bear this in mind as you plump out the foliage framework with flowers, using one colour at a time. Remember, the brightest colours give the most emphatic line. Hold the flowers lightly against the container to assess stem heights. Set the tallest flowers in position at the tallest point, following the height of the branches. Trim the stems as you go.

If the flowers droop their heads or topple to the sides, you will need to trim the stems further to make them the right height for the container support. However, irregularity is part of the charm; never be too contriving, but let the flowers fall into place.

Add other colours to harmonize with, or contrast against, this arrangement. Perhaps you are working

in a monochrome palette of all-white flowers, in which case you should consider varying the foliage to heighten the whites with silvery grey leaves. Or perhaps you are planning a duotone arrangement, as here. In a flamboyant mix of many colours, you may distribute the colour hues evenly; or, if you prefer, use bold accent colours in certain spots to pick up a swirl of colour on a ceramic container or to emphasize other flower colours. In any scheme it is always worth testing whether an accent would improve the effect – perhaps a lime-green flower, or a white one, or a sprig of grey leaves. Take time to experiment and consider the effects you wish to achieve while respecting the natural line and form of the flowers.

The photographs on these pages show three stages in the gradual build-up of a composition. The starting-point was a casual windowsill line-up of two plain blue ceramic vases, two lidded pots, a red jug and a blue coffee pot. First, the foliage frame was created, using *Stephanandra,* **fennel heads and geranium leaves, evenly distributed. The fennel stalks were placed to cross the divide between the two vases, reaching out over the low pots. Then (second picture), orange monbretia was added for contrast, the stalks left untrimmed to carry the colour high above the green foliage and away from the contrasting container colours. Lastly (third picture), blue cornflowers were added for a vibrant contrast with the orange. These flowers were trimmed with scissors to make the specks of blue dance between the bold orange and the container hues.**

MASSED DISPLAYS

Armfuls of flowers in banked colours tumbling from a vase make a strong focal point in any room. These lavish displays are relatively simple in their impact and are easy to arrange, provided that you use the flowers in abundance. Even humble weeds can be transformed from garden irritants to interestingly lavish bouquets if massed indoors.

Everyone has their own inspiration when massing flowers. You can restrict yourself to only one colour range within the same species – for example, boughs of lilac spilling from a china pitcher or bunches of ranunculus deepening from palest yellow to orange. Or alternatively, you can mix many different hues. Bunches of sweet william ringed with clove carnations and old-fashioned pinks will conjure up the herbaceous border in a country garden. For an interplay of form, colour and texture on a giant scale, you could draw inspiration from the flower paintings of 18th-century Dutch artists like Jan Hendrik Fredriks. In one of Fredriks' canvases, striped parrot tulips, white peonies, orange nasturtiums, hollyhocks in cream and gold, trailing blue

convolvulus, lacecap hydrangeas, purple larkspur and creamy roses, all in one vase, resolve their differences in a splendidly extravagant composition that is easy to copy today.

When planning a traditional mixed bouquet, look in the florist's store where pails of different flowers are set side by side; this will give you an immediate guide to the many combinations. Whatever the flowers, buy lots of them. It is the total effect that counts, not the brush strokes. Build

up living colour from the outline of branches or sprays that radiate from the container. Stand back and fill the space with sprays. The outline could spread horizontally in a long, low arrangement, or radiate upwards like the spokes of a wheel, or maybe take a rounded, compact form. The trick is to build up the shape when you place the flowers within the broad outline. Group blooms for contrasts of shape and colour. As you add more flowers, the stems will hold each other in

position quite firmly.

The container must be large enough to hold a quantity of flowers in a sufficient depth of water; its diameter should be at least half the diameter of the arrangement. Large quantities of flowers will drink water thirstily, so you will need to top up daily. Some of the blooms will fade faster than others: when the massed arrangement is past its best, remove the faded flowers and divide up the rest into smaller nosegays.

Paradoxically, massed flowers are easier to assemble than simple groups. It would be hard to make any bunch totally devoid of charm. Yet some skill is needed to balance blooms with other shapes and colours. Also, you need to know when to stop: each bloom should retain its individual grace, as in this fishtank arrangement composed of borage, Queen Anne's lace, bluebells, white *Spiraea* and green-flowered *Helleborus foetidus* and *Euphorbia robbiae*.

To preserve unity in a massed bunch, it helps to choose flowers that have the same form, as in this window display. Tall spires of astrantia, green *Sedum* and blue gentian, mixed with catmint and wild oats, berberis, poppy seed capsules and tuberoses all radiate evenly from the narrow neck of the speckled vase.

A SENSE OF PROPORTION

You can be excessive with flowers. The more flowers, the more theatrical the effect. But to keep a sense of proportion, you must bear in mind not only the scale of the rooms in which they are to be displayed, but also the scale of the containers. Clearly, tall delphiniums set in a squat bowl become ungainly, just as full lacy caps of hydrangeas spilling from a small base look top-heavy.

The width and height of the flowers in relation to the container size are crucial factors. If they appear bunched, you will need to divide the group between two vases. Too tall, and you will need to trim the stalks: cut off a little at a time. If the stems are already too short, so that the petals just peer above the rim of your chosen container, you do not necessarily need a shallower one – instead you could add some long-stemmed flowers, leaving the lower flower heads in place as a form of ground cover.

To extend the proportions of an arrangement, you do not have to build up dense massing. Just one or two tall stems or branches will serve to increase the height, or you can lengthen the display by using trailing foliage.

Patterning on the container will play a part in the apparent proportion. A small-scale, busy pattern will tend to make a vase or bowl look smaller in relation to an identically-sized container of a bolder design. Colour, perhaps surprisingly, also affects apparent size: an "advancing" colour, such as red or orange, will tend to make a vase look smaller than one in a "receding" colour, such as blue.

Below: **Although there is a dramatic contrast of scale here, it is kept within bounds by the spreading stems of Solomon's seal curving protectively over two little pots holding alkanet, bluebells, ixia and *Euphorbia robbiae.***

Left: **The jar of gerbera daisies (below) can stand alone but also has a place in a more complex display in which contrasts of proportion play a major role. The tall slender glass vase displaying massed green stalks of tuberoses dominates the daisies and zinnias. Yet the two patches of colour – red/orange and green/white – are disposed in roughly equal proportions.**

Below: **Flower stalks can be trimmed so that the mass of colour balances the visual weight of the container, as in this example. The shapely bronze-effect jar with its slender base widening to a bulbous neck has the same outline as the flowers above, which similarly widen upwards and outwards.**

The lines of furniture can sometimes suggest a flower arrangement. In this display, delphiniums and whitebeam in the tallest vase continue the slant of the table leg – an effect echoed on a smaller scale by the flowers in the square glass tank to the right. Notice also how the crossed stems in the end vases repeat the central joint of the table supports.

In the fashion world, hemlines drop or rise, lapels broaden or narrow. This is all a matter of line. The designer with flowers, no less than the fashion designer, needs an appreciation of line in any composition. The way that flowers grow naturally dictates the line. Even seemingly casual bunches, if they are successful, depend on linear harmony.

The precise approach you take will vary according to the flowers you want to display. Sometimes the arrangement will be compact and rounded, with umbels of Queen Anne's lace, fennel and dill. Sometimes, the overall effect will be narrow and vertical; or radial, with spires and branches splaying outward in a fan shape. In a mixed bunch, linear characteristics – for example, arching sprays of flowering shrubs – can be used as exclamation marks that capture attention.

Sometimes a respect for the natural line means letting a bough or spray stand alone. Tropical exotica often merit this exclusivity – the cattleya orchid, for example.

When considering line, allow for the movement of flowers. Some, such as tulips, actually grow and shift position swayingly inside the vase. The grape hyacinth is one of a whole group of flowers that droop gradually under the weight of the heavy heads, presenting an intriguingly changing display.

Flowers can be inspired by container shapes. A glass fish bowl holds a group of flowers chosen for the same rounded form – anemones, a single tulip and the white roses, all linked by the crisscrossing lines of the stems. Tolmiea leaves, with their dainty green markings, complete the effect.

STEMS

White bells of snowflake (*Leucojum*) are simply displayed here in two glass containers, with slanted stems below water level providing an interesting pattern and preventing the flowers from toppling. If you took a pencil and followed the outline of the bell-like flowers from left to right, the resulting pattern would be shaped like the plunge and soar of a bird on the wing. By trimming stems to different heights, you could reproduce this attractive shape in a single container.

Flowers and leaves are borne upon the stem that nourishes them: flower arrangers who hide stems are suppressing a vital part of the living plant. The stem should be considered as carefully as the flower for the line and form it adds to any arrangement.

Stems are either woody or soft. They may be knobbled and twisted like briars, or firm and straight to support many leaves. Some trail and bend, some have thorns, others, such as blue borage or poppies, bristle with fine hairs. Even awkwardly shaped stems are interesting – such as those of cottage garden sweet peas, which become long and curving as they strive to reach the light. Colours vary, too. The willow and the dogwood species, for example, include some attractive red and silvery stems.

For too long, stems have been hidden inside ceramic containers, impaled upon spikes that hold them rigidly in place. By stripping off leaves and using glass containers to expose the stems you can contrast their lines effectively with the flowers. To stiffen stems with artificial aids is the antithesis of sensitive flower arrangement; a little thought will reveal much more gentle and natural means of support. One way is to interlace stems to form a casual webbing. By slanting stems in parallel groups within the container, you can form an interesting oblique pattern below the waterline, as well as providing a loose trellis for upright-stemmed flowers.

When building up this kind of grouping, you need a container large enough to prevent too tight a clump of green stems. A two-tiered arrangement – below the waterline a solid green mass of upright stems all trimmed to the same height, above it a profusion of coloured blooms – always looks clumsy. The flowers will usually look better in a generously sized bowl.

The easiest way to display stems is to choose slender-stemmed plants such as sweet peas and set them in flask-necked glass containers. Then you do not have to create a firm base of stems to support heavy heads. The narrow necks will give support and prevent the stems from bending too much under their burden. Cluster these small containers in groups, and vary the shapes and sizes.

Plants with thick, soft stems, such as tulips, are more difficult, as the flower heads are larger and the arrangement will topple if not fitted firmly into a tall, wide-necked container. Glass cylinders, or simple square containers, are ideal for grouped arrangements of soft-stemmed flowers. Trim the stems to give some diversity in height and interlace them to provide support at the base, below water level.

Left: **Abstracting three of the individual components from the sweet pea arrangement shown above makes a more formal composition, with the emphasis on the two stems arching away from the soft stemmed *Helleborus foetidus*. The small matched jars flanking the sweet peas, create a pleasing symmetry that is best appreciated against a plain background.**

Above: **The unusually tall necks of these glass flasks squeeze sweet pea stems and whitebeam sprigs into vertical bands of green that anchor the composition, offsetting the sinuous curves. To give a pleasing outline to the arrangement and distribute the colourful flower heads at different heights, the stems have been trimmed to varying lengths. Making a major feature of the stems gives the sweet peas a dignity and presence that dominates the fuller flowers in the foreground.**

TEXTURES

Different leaves, stems, grasses and flowers offer the designer an infinite range of textures. Think of papery-thin Japanese anemones, feathery grasses, velvety roses, furry catkins and glossy tulips. In each of these examples, the adjective chosen summarizes a facet of the plant's character that is no less important than colour or form in defining the pleasure that plant gives to us. Of course, we do not need to touch plants to appreciate their beauty – eye-appeal is the basis of flower arranging. Nevertheless, we infer textures from appearances, and in a complicated way the visual aspects of a flower, leaf or stem evoke its feel. That is why using textures creatively, and combining them imaginatively, are vital ingredients of the flower designer's skill.

To draw attention to subtleties of textures, it's important to choose the right background. A woven silk or bark wallpaper makes a natural setting for a vase full of silken grasses. Pale woodwork beeswaxed to a golden patina will heighten the appeal of a mixed bunch from a country garden. A plain, unplastered brick wall makes a suitably rough-textured backdrop to the mellow glow of Canterbury bells or hollyhock spires. In contemporary high-tech settings, tulips are much favoured to carry through the theme of glossy, lac-quered surfaces. However, it is impossible to lay down rules about textural combinations, as so much depends on the individual character of your room.

Recognize the potential of everyday objects, or of your special, treasured collections, as receptacles and props that will bring fresh flowers to life. For example, a pleasing match might be obtained by pairing the milky fineness of the Japanese anemone with the pearly translucence of seashells; an icegreen guelder rose with an exquisite porcelain figurine; a pot of pansies with the rich velvet glow of an oriental carpet; or papery buttercups with a paper fan. On a bedside table you might choose an ivory-backed hairbrush to stand beside milky white Lenten roses, or in a bathroom blue scent bottles beside spires of blue delphiniums that are tall enough to be reflected in the nearby mirrors.

For a frankly theatrical and romantic still life, in which textural relationships play a crucial part, lay rose heads upon an old leatherbound book, so that the roughcut parchment pages echo the frills of the petals. Silk drapes can be used to underline the texture of glossier flowers, such as tulips – an approach that can look particularly sumptuous if you complete the high-sheen effect with a crackleglaze lustre vase.

Opposite, top: **A small display of treasured antiquarian books is looked at afresh with just two 'Queen Elizabeth' peach roses laid upon them in a throwaway gesture. The frilled petals evoke the pleasures of uncut pages, while the old leather bindings offer a textural contrast with the blooms.**

Opposite, bottom: **Setting rare mauve tulips among common lilac sprays heightens their waxy blooms by a subtle contrast of textures. Surrounding textures contribute immeasurably to the mood. The silken drapes and lovely pot marbled with gold make the simple bunch lavish.**

Right: **Translucent white marking on these frosted-glass bowls echo feathery fronds of love-in-a-mist. The pale heads have the same delicacy as the glass, appearing to float above the stems, which are glimpsed like underwater fronds below the waterline. There is great delicacy in the interplay of textures and simplicity of colour.**

MAKING THE MOST OF SCENT

Scent is an elusive, highly individual experience, which cannot be measured on any scale. Yet most people would agree upon the associations that scents conjure up: a bowl of sweet peas, for example, is enough to capture all the fragrance of a country cottage garden.

Pungent, spicy, honied, garlicky, balmy – these are some of the adjectives used to evoke the scents of different flowers or leaves. Yet many scents are unique, and defy such easy description. Wallflowers, for example, have their own special fragrance, with a hint of both jasmine and orange. The scent of violets is more elusive: in Shakespeare's words, "Forward, not permanent: sweet, not lasting, The perfume and suppliance of a minute."

The following section of the book offers some creative ideas for exploiting fragrances – from the sensuous richness of roses and lilies to the humble charm of the country nosegay.

This lavish bouquet mixes the heady fragrance of clustered blooms of stock with a scented white trumpet of *Lilium longiflorum*, pink-flushed *Spiraea* and 'Carte Blanche' roses. Place such bouquets near a seating area so that you can enjoy their scent while you spend some time relaxing.

TRADITIONAL ROSES

Until the 19th century, all roses flowered only once a year, either in early or late summer. The quest for repeated flowering through a complex process of interbreeding led to showier blooms, but often with some sacrifice in fragrance.

"Old roses" have recently enjoyed a revival, not only for their scent but also for their old-fashioned, full-blown appearance. There is 'Rosa Mundi', for example – the pale pink, crimson-striped hybrid of *Rosa gallica*, oldest of all garden roses. The alba roses (which include the superbly scented pale pink 'Maiden's Blush'

and 'Queen of Denmark') characteristically have grey-green leaves. Moss roses such as 'William Lobb' derive their name from a moss-like growth on the sepals and flower stalks. Although most of these old shrub roses are summer-flowering only, there are notable exceptions which flower again in autumn – for example, the old Bourbon rose 'Boule de Neige', with its silky ivory blooms.

The famous tea scent that rose lovers enthuse about originated in China. In the early 19th century, tea roses were imported to the West in the cargo holds of tea traders' vessels.

Although intolerant of frost and somewhat weak-stemmed, they were highly prized for their delicate blooms, exquisite fragrance and repeat flowering habit. Their marriage with hardier roses already established in the West began the long history of hybridization that yielded the modern hybrid teas.

Not all hybrid teas still have the tea scent, but most have some fragrance. Excellent choices for flower arrangements include red 'Fragrant Cloud', silvery pink 'Silver Lining', golden yellow 'Dutch Gold', pale pink 'Lady Sylvia', velvety red 'Mister Lin-

coln' and cream and red 'Double Delight'. 'Sutter's Gold', the most fragrant of all yellow roses, retains the tea scent to an exceptional degree.

For triumphant autumn colour, the hybrid musk roses are unrivalled. Especially fragrant examples are ivory-bloomed 'Prosperity' and apricot-pink 'Felicia'.

Floribunda roses are valued for their continuous flowering and the abundance of blooms, which make them ideal for cutting. A few are also scented – notably, pearly white 'Margaret Merill' and copper-coloured 'Fragrant Delight'.

When planning an arrangement of scented roses, take into account the room conditions. Fragrance depends on the release of essential oils, which is encouraged by a warm, humid atmosphere. If the room is cold, even the highly scented varieties will disappoint.

Far left: **Roses are romantic, their velvety blooms a traditional accompaniment to candlelit evenings. To convey this mood, a pair of engraved glass candlesticks has been set beside two glass bowls of roses. An unconventional touch is the sprinkling of wild oats in the left-hand container, their delicate, wispy forms contrasting effectively with the full-blown blooms.**

Left: **A bowl of old-fashioned roses captures the very essence of summer. Old-fashioned roses have recently enjoyed a revival of popularity. Here, deep pink roses dominate the foreground, and in the background there are more full-blown roses combined with buds and a sprinkling of tolmiea leaves. The fuller pale pink cabbage rose is deliciously fragrant.**

Below: **Dusky pink roses have a special glow in late-summer evening light. Here, the frilly petals of the central rose have opened to reveal the golden centre. Accompanying the roses to provide extra scent is the gold-banded** *Lilium auratum.*

LUXURIOUS LILIES

Right: **In any cottage bunch, *Lilium auratum* deserves its place, as each stem clusters more trumpets than any other lily.**

Below: **In this detail of a table centrepiece *Lilium regale* is teamed with green tassels of love-lies-bleeding (*Amaranthus* 'Viridis'), and pink hydrangea.**

Most prized for fragrance of all flowers except the rose, the lily has a regal bearing, coupled with a longevity that makes it particularly popular with flower arrangers.

One of the most valued of all lilies is the madonna lily (*Lilium candidum*), with its golden, pollen-bearing antlers and honey-scented sweetness. The orange flowers of *L. henryi*, clustered upon purplish-black stems, are also very fragrant. Some so-called lilies are not actually members of the *Lilium* family – for example, the pinkish Belladonna lily (*Amaryllis belladonna*), lily of the valley (*Convallaria majalis*), and the white St Bernard's lily (*Anthericum liliago*):

of these, only the lily of the valley is notably fragrant.

Lilies can be tucked into bouquets in the seemingly random way in which they grow in cottage gardens, or set alone in glass containers to be admired for their graceful form and fragrance. Glass is suitable for displaying lilies, as their stems are usually firm and elegant. Avoid over-elaborate containers, or they will detract from the perfect flower forms.

All lilies need careful handling and are best bought (or picked) in bud, as they will open well in water. The stems should be split and the base leaves removed. Avoid getting the heads wet, or the blooms will be spoiled.

Scented flowers are virtually essential in an otherwise unscented bunch. Solomon's seal has lovely bell-like flowers pendant upon curving stems, but no fragrance. So here I have teamed it with *Lilium auratum*.

Cooks appreciate the aromatic qualities of herbs more than florists do. Nevertheless, using fresh herbs in mixed flower bunches adds fragrance. They are decorative too – a quality that tends to be all too briefly admired on the chopping board before the herbs are shredded for garnishes. Many are evergreen, providing year-round foliage.

In a window box you can grow enough herbs for both the culinary and floral arts. You will need to trim new growth constantly between spring and autumn to prevent the plants from straggling and to encourage vigour.

Suitable choices for decorative display include the fern-like fronds of sweet cicely (green with a white underside), grey-green southernwood (*Artemisia abrotanum*), gold-and-green lemon balm (*Melissa officinalis* 'Aurea'), and sage, *Salvia* 'Purpurascens' with its purplish bloom; the leaves of these plants will scent a room if crushed a little and placed beside the fire or in a warm spot.

Some scented herbs are tall, reaching 6 feet (1.8m) – for example, bronze or green fennel, with its ornamental, aromatic seed heads and angelica, which brings a statuesque beauty to arrangements when it flowers with yellow-green umbels in its second year. Lovage's celery-like leaves are decorative in larger displays, as are branches of rosemary, with tiny blue flowers studded along the spikes.

Few herbs are notably colourful, even when in flower. The three principal exceptions are blue-flowering borage, red-bloomed bergamot and the yellow flowers of feverfew.

Herbs provide a fragrant framework into which a tapestry of cottage flowers can be woven. Even as their flowers or leaves fade, herbs retain their scent, which herbalists in medieval times found "piercing to the senses". This arrangement contains lavender-coloured catmint or *Nepeta* (which cats love to roll in) and flowering mauve garden mint with a giant leaf of lemon-scented geranium.

A sprig of lemon balm was traditionally included in a nosegay for its reviving fragrance. It features in the mixed bunch of spearmint and parsley in the larger bowl here. In the low bowl in the foreground there are viburnum berries. The yellow flowers are rue.

Left: **Scented flowers can conjure up country walks. Place a comfortable chair next to the flowers, so that you can savour their fragrance while you relax. Here, fragrant roses, pink, yellow and white, are mixed with flowering mint, scented honeysuckle and barberry.**

In a scented country garden, a haunting mixture of flowery fragrances fills the air. You can create a similar blend of perfumes indoors by arranging simple country-garden flowers in mixed bunches. In such bouquets, no one flower dominates.

The country garden collection of scented flowers includes buddleia, broom, clove carnations, honeysuckle, heliotrope, jasmine, garden lilac, night-scented stock, sweet peas, tobacco plant, violets and wallflowers, among others. Some smell strongest at dawn, others at dusk. Sometimes noonday sun is needed to release the essential fragrant oils that tempt the butterflies and bees. Outdoors, you need great beds of these flowers to scent the air. Yet picked and put in a vase, each flower will yield its scent more effectively in a confined space indoors.

Country gardeners appreciate that you produce more prolific flowering if you pick blooms consistently. Sweet peas picked as they flower will reward with more blooms in a later season.

When the petals drop, add them to a basic potpourri mixture bought commercially. Damask roses, acacia blossoms, clove pinks, mock orange, heliotrope, marigolds, leaves of verbena, lemon balm, rosemary leaves and mint are just some of the favourite ingredients. A mixture of powdered orris root scented with spices such as nutmeg will keep the leaves and petals sweet-smelling. Store the mixture in an airtight jar until the petals fade and the fragrance builds up.

The first description of sweet peas in England comes from the plant collector Dr Robert Uvedale in 1699. Uvedale identified a scent "somewhat like honey and a little tending to the orange flower smell". Here, sweet peas are bunched simply in a fish tank, although they can also be set in jugs with their tendrils and leaves.

FOOD AND FLOWERS

Food and flowers make a natural pairing – after all, they often grow together. You do not need a candlelit dinner to justify using flowers as a decorative accompaniment to a meal. Even simple daisies in a jug on the breakfast table are an improvement upon cereal boxes.

Flowers at mealtimes should be chosen to complement the colours of the food and table settings. As the following pages show, there are countless possibilities for exercising your wit and imagination.

Left: **Al fresco dining demands lavish flower arrangements to compete with the natural surroundings. On an old wooden table are baskets of flowers, which can be removed when it is necessary to make space for trays of food. The pink and mauve hydrangeas** provide delicate colour. **Damsons, greengages, black and green grapes and a basket of leaves complete the picture.**

Above: **Fruit with flowers in the same bowl make an unconventional but perfectly appropriate pairing. Here, blue** gentians bring a flashy brilliance to the darkening purple figs and grapes. **Purple anemone heads scattered throughout the fruit bowl are used to blend with the purples and, with the gentians, contrast sharply with the greens – their opposites on the colour wheel.**

A SENSE OF OCCASION

When planning a meal, it is worth putting as much thought into flowers as into recipes. However, there is no need for a starchy formality. Whatever the occasion, the flowers must be simply arranged to fall naturally, as they grow.

You can plan floral centrepieces round the menu, to colour-match with the food. Scarlet gerbera blooms and their fresh green leaves suit a simple red radicchio with an endive salad. Fronds of fennel with golden seed heads on tall stalks in a jug appropriately accompany platters of grilled fish with lemon.

Nouvelle cuisine has taught us to look afresh at the presentation of flowers with food. Leaves and stems, as well as flower heads, make suitable garnishes, both for individual plates and for the serving platter. The cook can take snips from window boxes, greenhouse-grown flowers or flowering shrubs out of doors, or split open exotic fruits to adorn the table. There are also blue borage flowers to float in summer drinks, aromatic leaves of sweet rocket to complement summer salads, and nasturtium seeds and flowers to add a peppery relish to a table setting.

China, tablecloth and flowers need to be considered together. Blue-and-white china is a favourite for table settings, as it provides a harmonious background for food. The three pictures on these pages show a well-composed scheme based on blue-and-white, with cream and green for contrast.

Above: **The blue delphiniums are sharpened by green *Stephanandra* leaves and creamy roses. The centrepiece is a platter of mange tout peas, green runner beans, curly endive, corn salad and red and yellow tomatoes. The cream cheeses are decorated with chervil and a few scarlet strawberries and anemones to provide supplementary colour.**

Above: **Brilliant blue
delphiniums were chosen
for their flower shapes
which are similar to the
decorative white flowers
painted on the blue
background of the plates.**

THE SURPRISE HELPING

The formality or informality of a meal will be determined by the table setting and the presentation of the food. Flower containers contribute to this mood. For example, earthenware bowls on a gingham cloth look much less formal than porcelain or crystal on white damask. At traditional occasions such as Christmas, you can take an individual approach – perhaps using cheerfully coloured flowers in glass jars, set among a basket of plums, tangerines and nuts, in place of the usual glitter.

When choosing flowers, take the tableware carefully into account. Plain white china can be given a pattern with individual flower heads laid upon each plate; and the same flower can be set in the table centrepiece. Sometimes, it is more fun to tone down a grand occasion with fresh meadow flowers, or a cornfield bunch of poppies and grasses. Little country garden flowers, meandering in a line along a formal rectangular table will attract more attention than the ubiquitous bunch of roses. Single flowers at individual place settings can be used as impromptu button-holes; or you can float flowers in a shallow bowl as part of the table centrepiece.

If the plates are already patterned

An alcove setting in which the flower choice has been inspired by the fabric patterns. Tablecloth, drapes and napkins have full-blown apricot flowers set on a pale turquoise background; so bluebells have been introduced for that same drift of blue and Iceland poppies in the same apricot, with hosta leaves and artichoke foliage as a foil.

with floral motifs, duplicate the effect with real flowers or foliage. Nasturtiums will echo the distinctive pattern of a Villeroy and Bosch dinner service, while willow fronds are suitable accompaniments for blue-and-white willow-patterned china.

Consider the height of the table arrangements. It is distracting to have to peer at guests through a forest glade of greenery and flowers. For conversations across the table, low bowls are not the only solution. An alternative is to choose long-stemmed florists' flowers and set them in a tall, slender vase, stripping away the leaves so that the centrepiece is a column of green which tumbles in a froth of leaves and flowers above the guests' heads. You can create this effect with marguerites: their grey-green foliage, white daisy-like flowers and firm, slender stems are invaluable for all table settings. For extra emphasis, add a few trailing plants spilling from the sides. At close quarters, flowers attract detailed attention, so be sure that each bloom is perfect.

Left: **Succulent green apples and green-tinged guelder roses enhance each other, evoking freshness and healthy living. A simple plain white bowl draws maximum attention to this somewhat novel pairing.**

Above: **A detail of the alcove setting illustrated on the opposite page. The crisscrossing stems in the fish tank make a deliberate contribution to the overall effect.**

GRACEFUL GARNISHES

When a table groans under the weight of too many dishes, an ornate bunch of flowers is usually the first object to be removed. On crowded tables you should maximize the space by keeping flower arrangements small and simple. This is the right approach for a tea table or tray, or for casual party meals on occasional tables. To avoid clutter, use a simple jug of flowers, or individual bouquets arranged on plates.

When space is at a premium, the wisest choice might be to treat flowers or greenery as discreet garnishing. Some vegetables, such as scarlet-bloomed runner beans, will provide tiny flowers that you can use to decorate plates. Similarly, mange touts can be teamed with flowering sweet peas of the same genus, or with strawberries for colour contrast – hardly delectable in gourmet terms, but certainly lots of fun. To a board of soft, milky cheeses, try adding horsechestnuts, split figs, dates or flower heads. The Victorian practice of adorning puddings with crystallized rose petals frozen in icing sugar falls into the same category.

Strawberry cake, a bowl of fruit and glasses of iced tea with slices of lemon offer plenty of colour for this midsummer tea party. The floral and foliage accompaniments can therefore be relatively muted – just lilac-coloured gypsophila with ixia, *Alchemilla mollis*, and mossy *Helxine* growing in an earthenware pot.

All four of these decorative plate arrangements are intended as feasts for the eye as well as for the palette. Anemones (accompanied by the zinnias on the cucumber sandwich plate) are the only inedible feature. Note the use of fresh herbs, the slices of kiwi fruit, and the contrasts of colour and texture on each plate – for example, red anemones and strawberries with purplish damsons.

EATING OUTDOORS

Casual meals eaten outdoors can be among the most memorable. It is often said that food tastes better in the open air. Flower arrangements can play a part in adding finishing touches to a patio or garden meal. However, they must be kept simple, as they are in competition with nature. Now is the time to judge the absurdity of wired, formal arrangements. You will want to free cut flowers from such restraints, keeping the natural grace that flowers show in the wild.

For outdoor eating, lay a sprig of blossom on the table or some herbal garnishes on each plate; position a basket or jug filled with a simple bunch of freshly picked flowers echo-ing the glories of the garden.

A charming touch is to encircle each napkin with a tendril of creeper, or a supple stem of honeysuckle, its white flower fragrant and decorative. Or embellish each place setting with an outline of creeper laid flat upon the table and dotted with flowers.

Crudités have an ornamental value as a centrepiece. Spikes of celery, white fennel, twigs of carrot, florets of cauliflowers, spring onion shoots and red radishes make a satisfying sur-round to a pot of sauce. On a hot day, curly cabbage, Chinese lettuce and red radicchio leaves, spiked with en-dive, in a bowl of iced water, look both cool and tempting.

Left: **This informal arrangement uses glass vases to trap the summer sunlight. Flowering chives and leaves of celery combine with rose-pink sprays of *Diascia* and pink campanula. The pinks harmonize with the radicchio leaves, and with the decorative ceramic lid at the right of the picture.**

Far left: **For outdoor tables, it make sense to use snippings and clippings from the garden, rather than florists' flowers. Set aside some time for exploring the garden to pick the best blooms. Here, I used hosta flowers, a single head of thrift, a little *Alchemilla mollis*, bergenia leaves and a handful of roses and white anemones.**

Above: **Outdoors you do not need to arrange flowers with quite the precision that you might apply to an interior arrangement. Choose a simple (but not necessarily plain) container, and fill it with a mixed bunch. This informal arrangement, in an appropriately floral jug, features hosta leaves, *Anemone japonica*, bergenia leaves and roses.**

INTERIORS

Flowers are always seen in the context of the overall decoration of the room. When creating flower arrangements, you need to consider the fabrics, wall coverings, carpets – even the furniture and ornaments – not just the colour, form, line and scent of the flowers and their relationship with the containers. By using flowers imaginatively, you can create a total mood – be it oriental splendour, country-cottage charm or city-apartment modernity.

The examples in the following section show the contribution that flowers can make to an interior design, and to the creation of an identifiable style. Many of the schemes illustrated are shown both in a broad view and in a number of close-ups. In some, Tricia Guild has been inspired by the richest designs of the past; in others, there is a graphic simplicity appropriate to many contemporary interiors.

Fresh flowers help to tone down the formality of this blue room, with its ornate carvings. As the basis for the flower colour, I picked out the coral that appears in the curtains, found garden roses to match, then added roses in other colours, using the green of tolmiea in the centre of the console table for contrast. Fennel stalks, mixed with powdery blue agapanthus, introduce height.

QUICK CHANGE

In some areas of design, the ability to make quick changes is crucial. Designers of store windows, for example, can transform the basic, never-changing backdrop with a few deft touches. Theatre designers know the importance of rapid scene changes to introduce a new location. Similar principles apply to interior designers who use flowers to add variety, and shifts of mood and emphasis, amid surroundings that remain static – at least until redecoration.

The best-planned interiors need flowers to provide finishing touches.

The smallest nosegay can reveal familiar objects in a new light. To make the most of the potential of flowers, you need to consider backgrounds carefully, and be alert to the possibilties you can create simply by rearranging the furniture, or moving ornamental objects.

If you have a favourite picture or poster, assess whether it might be worthwhile to move a table near it to support a flower arrangement in the same colours. Or you could open an antique folding desk top, or clear a space on a worktop, or move an occasional table under a pool of light

from a downlighter or floor lamp. All these options demand little more than a modest effort of the imagination – a willingness to be flexible. Look also at permanent features such as wallpaper and choose arrangements that will highlight colours or echo patterns. Familiar designs take on fresh life when flowers complement them. Apply this effort and the wealth of exciting quick changes will soon be recognized. The examples here and on the following pages show the advantages of an open-minded approach, whether the room is traditional or modern.

A change of flowers and accompanying ornaments can give a totally new look to the same piece of furniture. In the larger picture (far right) the traditional escritoire is decorated with a selection of blue-and-white china and a glass goblet filled with blue hydrangea heads and _Stephanandra_ leaves. Shifting the emphasis to the right and filling up the left side of the surface with a low group of fruitwood carvings and containers and old books makes you look more closely at the fretworked edges and overall shape of the cabinet (right). The objects have been carefully chosen to blend with a mellow glow of the furniture, instead of presenting a contrast, as did the blue-and-white china.

QUICK CHANGE

A modern print in black and yellow is the inspiration for two flower arrangements that are similar in mood yet radically different in colouring. In the left-hand arrangement I used a yellow vase whose colour and approximate shape correspond with the vase in the picture. Yellow flower heads and a dark brown sculptured dish echo the tones of the print, but the lilies add a contrasting pink. A low-key approach, which allows the picture greater dominance, is to use all-white containers and white gladioli (right).

FLORAL PROFUSION

This living room makes a virtue of floral excess – even the paintings are flower studies. By using flowers so unashamedly as the keynote, I aimed to create a strong sense of unity and bring the interior vibrantly to life. The other photographs on these two pages, and those on pages 114–15, show individual details of the scheme.

There is a grand profusion of flowers patterning the walls, windows and furniture in the sitting room scheme shown on these two pages. To use fresh flowers among such a riot of floral motifs demands a bold treatment – using massed bunches, not single blooms or gentle sprays. A vase of roses set upon an occasional table would be overlooked in this room, merging anonymously into the overall decorative theme; however, these large bouquets are the ideal choice for their surroundings, contributing to the colour scheme and helping to create a deliberate effect of floral extravagance.

Mixed bunches of country garden flowers in red, blue and purple balance with the decoration and distribute the main hues of the scheme equally around the room. Then, following the basic principles of flower design, accent colour is added. So the banks of massed magenta rhododendrons are offset by the introduction of a single ice-green guelder rose. The only accent colour that would be totally inappropriate in this room would be yellow, too warm to work alongside the colours from the crimson-blue range.

Scale is another important design consideration. The scale of flower arrangements should be carefully related to the scale of the surrounding fabric and wall patterns. Fresh flowers can emphasize the height and proportion of the pattern. For example, floral curtains whose patterns have a strong vertical emphasis may call for a tall vase of mixed country flowers placed on a console table beside them – any smaller, and the arrangement would risk being dwarfed by the pattern of the drapes.

Simple, plain rooms, lacking in notable architectural features, can be brought to life by fresh flowers artfully combined with multiple floral patterns. In this example, the room was tall, in the townhouse manner, but the scheme would translate just as easily into a small modern apartment. Contrary to the decorator's familiar maxim, patterned walls do not make rooms appear smaller. Co-ordinating floral patterns can unify a small room, instead of fragmenting the space as plain walls might. They can make a modest room look more imposing and add character to the most anonymous, box-like interior.

In an etched glass goblet (designed in the 18th century to hold celery), I arranged an informal spray of scarlet parrot tulips, pink alstroemeria, pink roses, delphiniums and Queen Anne's lace. All these flowers repeat in deeper tones the colours of the glazed chintz drapes behind them. The blue and gold French vase matches the period of the goblet and anchors the composition with cobalt blue.

FLORAL PROFUSION

A close-up of one corner of the living room described and illustrated on the previous two pages. The flowers were chosen to repeat the colours of the decorative background, but in more intense tones. In the low bowl there is richly toned azalea with a flecked mauve alstroemeria. The tallest vase contains apple blossom, delphiniums and the 'Stargazer' lily, with a single caladium leaf whose plum centre picks up the colours of the containers and the Oriental shawl at the right of the picture. A smaller vase holds delphiniums and a pink rose. Guelder roses, in all three arrangements, supply a unifying accent colour.

This picture closes in further on the bowl arrangement of azaleas, alstroemeria with lime green guelder roses (*Viburnum opulus*) to add lively accent colour to this magenta bowl holding pink blooms.

Two parrot tulips dominate this coffee table arrangement, with single heads of delphinium flowers stripped from the stalk and the green guelder rose.

TRANSFORMING THE TRADITIONAL

A challenge facing the interior designer is to combine the old with the new. Anyone who inherits some old pieces of furniture yet favours modern furnishing schemes knows the problem. It is an exercise in balance. The transient yet timeless beauty of fresh cut flowers will link the traditional and the contemporary. Use flowers lavishly, dotted about the room to draw attention to individual items and unify the scheme. A single bowl of flowers is insufficient in a room full of colour. Displays placed around the room will spread the flower colour add to the air of studied calm and

elegance, and prevent a traditional room from appearing too impersonal.

In traditional interiors, a formal corsage, wired and rigid, is often set in an urn upon a pedestal. While such a practice might be in keeping with the period, the treatment could only serve to make any modern furnishings in the scheme look completely out of place, and waste the potential of the flowers for creating a spontaneity. To bring new life and vigour to a relatively formal room, it is much better to allow flowers to trail and spill in abundance as they usually do in the garden.

All three pictures here show details of the luxuriously furnished living room featured on pages 106–107.

Below left: **Scented midsummer roses have a velvety bloom that is right for grand interiors such as this one. Together with candles and fruit (shown in the detail at far right), they create a composition inspired by 18th-century still life paintings.**

Below: **This romantic centrepiece is based on a deliberate contrast of scale. Just behind and to the right of the roses is a tall vase of smaller-scaled, paler flowers accompanied by delicate foliage – pale blue agapanthus, fennel stalks, a dark green *Bocconia* leaf and *Eremurus*. Look again at the broader view of this room (pages 106–107) to see how this echoes a similar juxtaposition in the boldly patterned drapes and the more delicate lining curtains behind.**

Right: **Another view of the tablescape illustrated at far left. Fruit and roses are used together to convey a mood of old-world abundance, with a casualness that suits the modern patterned fabrics.**

EASTERN NOSTALGIA

Left: **The turquoise-coloured chair coverings in Robin Guild's eastern-style living room have set the colour note for the flowers, with vibrant contrasts provided by curry plant, yellow-flowering fennel and pink hydrangeas. The green tolmiea on the pedestal appropriately suggests the 19th century.**

In the living room in Robin Guild's London home, ornately carved armchairs made by craftsmen in India at the turn of the century evoke another age and another continent, in contrast to the modern feel of the rough-panelled walls. The trunks used as occasional tables reinforce the atmosphere of antiquity and travel, as well as providing a surface for flower arrangements. In relatively confined surroundings such as these, textures become more noticeable than they would in a more spacious room, so it is a good idea to introduce rich textural contrasts among the foliage and flowers.

Above: **The arrangement on top of this well-travelled trunk provides a wealth of textures, as well as varying foliage shades, including silky grey lavender-cotton.**

Left: **In this chimneypiece arrangement, the turquoise vases and the background colour of the framed picture pick up the chair coverings at the far side of the room. Another shade of blue is contributed by love-in-a-mist, which contrasts with white flowers – 'Snow Princess' lilies, spires of white stock, daisy-like camomile and the tiny white stars of greenhouse-grown *Bouvardia*.**

DINING ROOMS

When space is at a premium, as it tends to be in modern apartments, the separate dining room is the first to be sacrificed. Today we live in the age of the kitchen-diner. However if you are fortunate enough to have a separate dining room with a table that is used only for occasional entertaining, you have a perfect location for lavish flower displays. Combine bold colours in bold containers. There is no reason why you shouldn't take up most of the table space, leaving just a narrow shelf around the edge.

Above right: **I believe that a bare dining table has a somewhat expectant air, as if waiting for something to happen – so I will fill the table with vases of flowers to create a large-scale still-life. Here, there is a deliberate balance between dark and light. From left to right in the six containers are _Thalictrum_ leaves, mixed sweet peas, _Anemone japonica_, green bells of Ireland and, in the last three arrangements, sweet peas mixed with variegated grasses and asparagus ferns.**

Right: **Glass tables reflect the containers – and even the flowers themselves if the angle of view is steep enough. Colour and pattern, therefore, make a double impact.**

A JOLT OF COLOUR

The photographs here show my own house in Chelsea, London, with its scheme of ivory and cream accented with flowers and with splashes of colour from fabrics, decorative detailing, occasional furniture and small-scale decorative objects. Although the room is plain, the flowers and objects all work together to create the effect of a busy pattern.

Left: When the background colour is neutral, discreet accents will stand out clearly. In this living room the white arum and *regale* lilies in a tall vase on the chimneypiece pick up the overall colour theme of the white walls and woodwork and the flowers in the modern painting behind. For extra colour, I added pink lilies to the vase.

Right: Flower accents and restrained decorative touches such as the charcoal trim on the blinds and the colourful scatter cushions contribute a wealth of visual interest to this cream study. On the chimneypiece are ranunculus and a tall pot of *Clivia* with stems of young maple leaves. On the table beside me, a glass cube holds ranunculus; and there are cream tulips behind. On the wicker table there is a jug of magnolia leaves with green arum lilies.

Right: A glass-topped table in a narrow hallway makes minimum demands upon space. I filled the vases with blossom (cherry, flowering quince and blackthorn) to take the eye upward. Such narrow spaces need vertical arrangements, not broadly spreading horizontal ones.

GRAPHIC SIMPLICITY

Modern rooms, bare of architectural detailing, are perhaps the most difficult to furnish with flowers. Space and proportions are different from those in more traditional rooms – not least because modern architecture usually reduces room size and ceiling height. So you must consider the vertical lines and horizontal spread of your flower arrangements with great precision.

In a typically contemporary interior, decisive flower choices are needed, as the background will usually be either plain, or emphatically patterned. Flower compositions need to be equally graphic. You need to balance the decorative features with great sensitivity, using flowers to embellish spaces that would otherwise be chillingly bare. Normally, there will be fewer flowers in a modern interior: restraint is preferable to the lavish use of bouquets.

A single bloom, or a single species, grouped in a plain glass cube, is a simple but effective choice. Within a species, you can add subtlety by choosing different colour tones, and by adding leaves for texture. A broader approach is to choose different flowers of the same colour. For example, you could take just ten red flowers – including, perhaps, poppy, cosmos, geranium and salvia. Seen from afar, outdoors, these blooms would become a drift of colour; but close up, in a plain interior, differences of form, colour and texture will stand out clearly.

Right: **This small modern apartment has wavy vertical stripes on the blinds, screens and sofa covering, which contrast with the geometry of the table supports. The flowers have been arranged to take up the crisscrossing theme, which is stated too by the oblique brushstrokes of the modern paintings on the window wall. On the low tables is a mixture of ixia, 'Stargazer' lily, and alstroemeria.**

Above left: **A close-up of the central arrangement in the room shown at right. Even the stork motifs of the twin blue jars are crisscrossed, like the slanted arum stems. The unusual angular tray holds a 'Rubrum' lily.**

A wall mirror doubles the impact of flowers in the bedroom shown opposite (top). There are sprays of pink spiraea, single and double stocks, lilies and country garden roses.

Luxury is important in the bedroom, no matter how restricted the space. A comfortable bed, with invitingly soft fabrics all around, is the perfect retreat. After fabrics, introduce flowers in restful pastel colours, with scented blooms.

Bedside tables are always low-level, which means that bedside flower arrangements will be gazed down upon. Compactly rounded arrangements, which can be viewed from all sides, are most satisfactory. Containers should have firm bases, to avoid the risk of your tipping them over when switching off the bedside light.

Keep bedroom arrangements relatively simple, unless you have a room on a really grand scale. Contrasting colours tend to be too lively for most bedrooms, so limit your colour palette and aim for a harmonizing scheme, with flowers echoing the fabrics.

The formality of a draped white and grey bedroom with fragrant flowers – roses, scented jasmine and, in the foreground, more roses with *Lilium longiflorum*, stocks and white lilac. A few sprigs of Queen Anne's lace have been dotted here and there.

Below left: **A country-fresh charm has been brought to this bedroom dressing table by pale pink stocks, apple blossom and small roses, all floating in an angular ceramic container, which looks rather like an ornate miniature lily pond.**

BEDROOMS

Above left: **Roses are seldom appreciated for their foliage and hips. But in this attic bedroom I snipped the leaves and green hips from country garden roses to emphasize the leafy outline on both the tablecloth and scatter cushion.**

Above: **A day bed, screened with drapes so that it resembles a four-poster, makes an attractive self-contained feature next to the window wall of a spacious bedroom. A restrained flower arrangement helps to mark the divide between the two distinct areas of the room. The real tulips complement the design of the fabrics, with anemones on the left.**

Right: **In this bedroom, dusky pastels recreate the soft glow of an interior by the French painter Vuillard. Pink and white hydrangeas are mixed with flat-topped *Eupatorium purpureum*, pink tassels of bridewort (*Spiraea salicifolia*) and blue love-in-a-mist (*Nigella*).**

Solomon's seal, *Cornus* 'Elegantissima' or variegated dogwood and early spring beech makes a welcoming bunch upon a hallway trunk (left) with bluebells, grasses and leaves in the jugs at the far right

Left: **Hallway flowers should be welcoming, but avoid stiffly formal bunches, which have associations of a reception desk. Rather, place flowers and foliage casually amid the everyday clutter that halls accumulate. Here, old leather cases and umbrella containers are enlivened by the pinks of *Eupatorium*, *Anemone japonica* and bridewort, yellow chrysanthemum and camomile daisies.**

Below: **An impromptu nosegay brings life to a group of potpourri holders, designed to fill a hallway with fragrance as the petals dry. A lavish bunch of colourful flowers could have made the potpourris appear particularly faded, so I used just a few annual chrysanthemums, snapdragon-like *Mimulus* and some geranium leaves.**

The entrance in every house should greet both owners and guests with the pleasure of something unexpected – as well as with happy memories. Fresh flowers are ideal for bringing that element of change to familiar surroundings.

Don't allow the hall to become a lifeless area to be passed through, or a mere repository for coats, hats and umbrellas. If there is space, enliven the area with a table and fresh flowers daily. To benefit most from floral displays, try to ensure that there is good natural light, and that artificial lights throw no gloomy shadows.

In houses that are short of space, the hall may become an important storage place – perhaps with bookshelves, or a trunk to house games, winter garments or tools. With a little initiative, you can satisfy such practical requirements and at the same time create a setting for an attractive flower display. A trunk, for example, may offer a flat surface suitable for vases or bowls, and the look of bookshelves will be improved if you use flowers to create a breathing space between rows of volumes.

Enhance the style of your hall by choosing the right container. A tall urn might be ideal for a black-and-white chequerboard floor. For a flagstoned cottage floor, you could choose baskets, while terracotta tiles might call for an unglazed earthenware tub or blue-and-white china upon wooden tables.

GARDEN ROOMS

Left: The window wall in this conservatory is grandly decorated with a festoon blind, instead of the usual outside awning, to preserve continuity with the rest of the interior. The ranunculus and the 'Peach Blush' lilies to the far right pick up the apricot of this blind, thus linking the two halves of the room. Notice, too, how the apricot backdrop highlights the tall maple in its floor-level container.

Below: Wicker surfaces in a garden room are suitably casual and summery. Here, I used a large hamper as the support for two arrangements that present a dramatic contrast of heights – 'Peach Blush' and 'Mont Blanc' lilies with silver birch in the tall glass cylinder and, in the glazed vase, ranunculus, *Euphorbia robbiae* and spiky hosta leaves. To unify the composition, I took two more lilies, cut short the stems and placed them in the left-hand vase.

Right: On this low table, cheerful 1920s pots set the tone and demand a bold choice of flowers, foliage and fruits. Amid geranium leaves, yellow yarrow and scarlet nerine stand out clearly. A shallow bowl holds tomatoes and lovage leaves. Strawberries with greengages, limes and green grapes continue the primary colours, but in the tall vase I have used more delicate colours, with variegated hosta and cyclamen, for variety.

Sun lounges, conservatories, glassed-in terraces and other kinds of garden room, whether used as dining areas or living areas, link inside and outside, dissolving the boundaries between the two. A similar effect is created if the living room has french windows, with a view of the garden beyond. Fresh flowers make the link more gracious and give a garden room a special presence, emphasizing the connection not only with the world outside but with the adjoining interior. To avoid making the garden room seem isolated, choose flowers and furnishings to complement the main interior, so that the outer room is seen as an extension of the inner.

WINDOW TREATMENTS

Window ledges used for flower displays link the flowers with the view beyond. This is true even of an urban apartment on an upper floor, without patio, terrace, or garden: the sky provides a changing backdrop to a bowl of flowers. Sometimes, creepers on the exterior wall can become part of an arrangement – distanced by the panes.

Usually, there will be only a narrow space between the window pane and the edge of the ledge, so to compensate for lack of depth you will need an arrangement based on vertical lines. Lavish bouquets will take up too much room and obstruct the view.

Key in the flower colour to the window drapes. Floral drapes can suggest the colour mix for a bunched display, and any accent colour in the trimmings – curtain tie-backs, piping and so on – can be echoed in the flowers. If the drapes are ornate, it may be effective to contrast them with the casual simplicity of grasses and hedgerow pickings. On the other hand, plain blinds may be enhanced by exotic blooms such as orchids.

A window is like a picture frame, highlighting the statement that a flower arrangement makes. Keep that statement positive: a simple treatment is usually best.

Above left: **Asymmetrical drapes in a soft floral pattern frame a country garden assortment, including mauve sweet peas and bunches of arching grasses.**

Above: **A close-up of the same window table arrangement shows sweet peas, grasses and scabious in the large glass goblet overhanging smaller groupings that continue that same colour theme.**

Shutters at a window create a background of horizontals which makes a dramatic contrast with the bunched flowers. Here, country garden flowers – pear and elder blossom, guelder rose, a few roses with buds and variegated ivy – are simply placed in a glass cube.

A shuttered window with slats of bleached wood provides a rectilinear background for this rounded arrangement. Dappled grey-green cyclamen leaves, lime-green tolmiea and a spherical mauve head of hydrangea spill from a blue glazed bowl. A single lime-green zinnia punctuates the compact form with its acidic sharpness. Rising from the low base are four long stems of hedgerow purple mallow: these take the display out of the commonplace, providing the verticals that counterbalance the horizontal slats. Place your finger over the mallow heads to see how much the composition loses: the loss of height reduces the display to an unexciting mound.

Opposite: **Only a heavy beam draws the eye toward this white-painted window area in a country cottage, decorated without drapes. Such simplicity demands a similar restraint in the choice of flowers: ornate blooms in a massive bowl would be overpowering. Instead, I chose only delicate flowers in a line-up of flower-patterned lustereware vases and bowls, two of which are left empty. Taking central place is a pot of blue cornflower. Then comes tall yellow yarrow, a snip of green pokeweed and *Phytolacca* towering over a scented collar of geranium leaves. A sudden drop to the compact bowl of begonia leaves brings a stop to the arrangement. The long line of receptacles has the effect of widening the window visually, while the tall flowers increase its apparent depth – though without blocking the view since the flowers are so delicate.**

FLOOR-LEVEL ARRANGEMENTS

This floor arrangement uses a heavy container placed well away from circulation areas, so that there is little danger of it being accidentally knocked over. Hedge snippings of golden privet are set among licorice-scented fennel. The cones scattered on the floor continue the countryside theme.

Although houseplants are often set in pots and tubs at floor level, fresh-cut flowers are seldom used in the same way. This is a pity, as floor-level arrangements offer a new angle on cut flowers, as well as an attractive way to fill unused space in an interior.

The containers do not have to be grand, like Chinese ginger jars. Equally, you can use baskets filled with country flowers (nourished by water in a plastic bag tied with twine around the stems). Stalks of fennel set in a narrow-necked umbrella stand can make an imposing display suitable for entrances. Always be sure to place the container where there is little likelihood of it being knocked over – especially if there are children in the home.

Scale and proportion are important. The container must not be disproportionate to the room. However, once you have identified a suitably sized container, there is virtually no limit to the plants that you can stand in it. Branches pruned from the garden, perhaps bearing autumn berries, can be made to stand eye-catchingly tall; but if you wish you can emphasize width rather than height. Certainly, you do not need giant plants of the prize-winning kind. Instead, you can create a horizontally spreading bunch from short-stemmed flowers, provided that you can fit a suitable lining inside the neck of a tall container.

Floor-standing containers filled with flowers can transform the dullest corner. In this hallway, I have used plumes of *Macleaya*, green bells of Ireland, leaves and berries of *Hypericum* and white scented tuberose. The height of the arrangement leads the eye toward the upper storey, and casts interesting shadows on the plain wall.

TABLESCAPES

A tablescape is a small still-life collection on a table top, with objects and flowers related to each other both by colour and by texture. By setting flowers, foliage and, sometimes, fruit among objects that you collected long ago, you enliven these objects, so that you can appreciate them afresh.

The choice of items for display will depend on the overall style you aim to create. Scented nosegays or mixed country bunches go well with fruitwood or enamelled boxes, and blue-and-white china. Or, instead, you can interpret the grand styles of the past – perhaps using an old leatherbound book or candleholders to reinforce the historic impression. Remember to take account of the table's immediate surroundings – for example, chintz drapes or a gilded mirror might make an effective backdrop to a nostalgic tablescape. A well-planned table arrangement should make the point collectively, yet each item should retain its individuality.

The flowers must be properly scaled in relation to the total picture: large Canterbury bells, for example, would probably dwarf a collection of miniature enamelled boxes, whereas scented lily of the valley would enhance them. If you have a low occasional table with a decorative top – such as marquetry, or a hand painted marbled finish – choose containers or flowers to echo the pattern, and make sure that enough of the table surface is visible to complete the composition.

Left: **A low-level tablescape designed to look good from above. The petals of the 'Rubrum' lily and tawny-pink alstroemeria are both speckled with markings upon their waxy petals. Also included are greenish bells of Ireland, like wisps of tissue on stems, and ixia, also in the small vase to the left. The flower markings match the marbled effect of the modern table, while the old volumes create an atmosphere of faded antiquity which highlights the flowers' freshness.**

Below: **No two flowers are repeated in the four arrangements that make up this window table display: only the containers' shape and colour unify the whole. The tallest vase contains *Macleaya* and fine larkspur, followed by a vase of roses, then grasses, and finally *regalum* and *auratum* lilies. The peachy flowers match the curtains.**

Left and left above: **Most artificially wired arrangements are designed to be viewed only from the front – an approach that can never work for low tablescapes, which need to be viewed** from all sides, and from above. This grouping of regal lilies, *Macleaya*, speckled alstroemeria, a rose and astrantia shows the advantages of a compact, rounded composition for occasional tables.

TABLESCAPES

Far right: **An old wooden table, bleached and scrubbed, provides a simple kitchen setting for a country-garden still-life. The objects are plain tools of the kitchen – a rudimentary candlestick, wooden salt cellar, butter churn and sieve. These humble objects are freshened with blue hydrangea and cornflowers with dark-eyed yellow chrysanthemum, marshy yellow mallow and a feathery grey frond of lavender-cotton.**

Right: **The mellow colours inlaid in a marquetry table have suggested the simplest foliage in this window arrangement – leaves of rheum and iris, combined with oak leaves in the adjacent Kashmiri bowl. The greenery restates the theme of the parkland beyond the window.**

Below: **Here, the same marquetry table** (shown at right) **has been used with lilies, trimmed to fit little pots. The flowers pick up the decorative motifs on the table surface.** *Stephanandra* **leaves, still summery green before the first frosts, make the lilies glow by contrast. The tablescape contains dramatic juxtapositions – rough with smooth, simple with ornate.**

TABLESCAPES

An inlaid border on this table frames a solidly patterned container in blue and white with a sprinkling of deep blue flowers. The hydrangea heads have been chosen to match these patterns – both table edge and container – creating an echo of shape and colour. They are accompanied by a little yellow fennel, some yellow dotted mignonette and leaves of oak, *Stephanandra* and *Thalictrum*.

Above: **Country pickings in
a pretty blue-and-white jug
with love-in-a-mist,
cornflowers and scabious
in variations of blue,
together with contrasting
Queen Anne's lace.**

Left: **The circular table and
two vases in this display
are unified by turquoise,
which binds together the
rich variations in material
and patterning. In the large
glass vase I used thistle
with phlox, hydrangea and
phytolacca, while the
smaller pot contains more
phytolacca, one green
zinnia, cyclamen leaves,
and knotweed. Observe
how the larger
arrangement blends with
the smaller one, blurring
the distinction between
them.**

AROUND THE FIREPLACE

A fireplace is the focal point that attracts most attention in a room. It is therefore an effective area to display flowers and foliage (although in winter flowers will not last long). On a chimney piece shelf you can either cluster a flower collection in groups of small pots or arrange them evenly in a long line-up. Even small numbers of flowers are enough to make an impact: for example, it is effective to limit the line-up to single flower heads in individual bud vases.

Fireplaces of brick or stone have a deliberately rough-hewn effect, but others are decoratively finished or detailed – perhaps marbled, hand-carved, handpainted or punctuated with ornamental tiles. Let the finish determine the flower colour.

In a traditionally furnished period room, a symmetrical arrangement might be appropriate, especially if the decoration is comparatively formal. If there is a central mirror over the fireplace, use a handsome pair of matching vases, one on either side.

In spring or summer, an empty hearth can be as cheerless as ashes. If you have a floral screen to hide the mouth of the fireplace, identify the flowers that are depicted and try to find corresponding real flowers to set on the shelf above.

Imitation marble on this contemporary fireplace is warmed up with pink 'Rubrum' lilies, white *regalum* lilies in bud, spires of larkspur and delphiniums, and little green spurge. The tall flower spikes bridge the evenly paced pair of mirrors, breaking up the regularity, as do the tiny glass bud vase and rounded bowl.

Left: **Flowers can be used to soften the rigid horizontals of the chimneypiece and to link it with a framed picture on the chimney breast. These three vases in emphatically modern colours contain** *Alchemilla mollis*, **green bells of Ireland, agapanthus, astrantia and scabious.**

Left: **Flowers near a fire need replacing daily, which can be an extravagance. Instead, I often use leaves, which can readily be renewed from hedges, trees and houseplants. Although there are only** three species here – St John's wort, *Thalictrum* and tolmeia – the effect is one of plenty.

Above: **A detail of the fireplace foliage arrangement shown at left. The berries of St John's wort, reddening in late autumn, will take on rich glowing colour in the light from a blazing hearth.**

CHOOSING AND CARING FOR FLOWERS

There is a vast repertoire of plants with special qualities that make them ideally suited for indoor display. This is not necessarily just a matter of the colour or form of the blooms. Other features with special appeal to arrangers are attractive foliage, tall, smooth stems strong enough to lift the flower heads high above the container, or berries for autumn or winter colour.

Pages 156 to 186 form an illustrated collection of some of Tricia Guild's own favourites, ranging from country garden flowers to snippings from trees and shrubs, flowering and non-flowering alike. The section ends with practical advice on cutting and conditioning, and on ways to bring forward the season of bulbs, blossom and foliage for winter arrangements.

A mixture of foliage and scented country garden flowers seldom fails to please. The woody stems of the roses and honeysuckle in this basket were crushed to improve their water intake. The finished arrangement is shown on page 94.

THE COUNTRY GARDEN

Traditionally, a small portion of the country garden was set aside for cutting flowers. The prize blooms could be gathered before the summer sun rose, to fill the rooms indoors with their freshness. Many gardens today lack the space for such an area, but the same plants can be grown in the herbaceous border, or set among vegetables in a small cottage plot.

Favourites include the azure delphiniums, blowsy peonies and poppies, spires of lupins and hollyhocks, and the more retiring pinks and pansies. The odd exotic may be cultivated for the challenge it presents, but the favourites shown here are the hardy perennials, tried and true, with a liberal scattering of annuals for their ephemeral brightness.

Agapanthus P
Agapanthus africanus
Sometimes known as African lily, the agapanthus flowers in late summer and thrives in sunny, sheltered spots. With its compact head of deep blue flower umbels set upon a tall smooth stem, uninterrupted by foliage, the agapanthus is ideal for cutting and arranging indoors.
▼

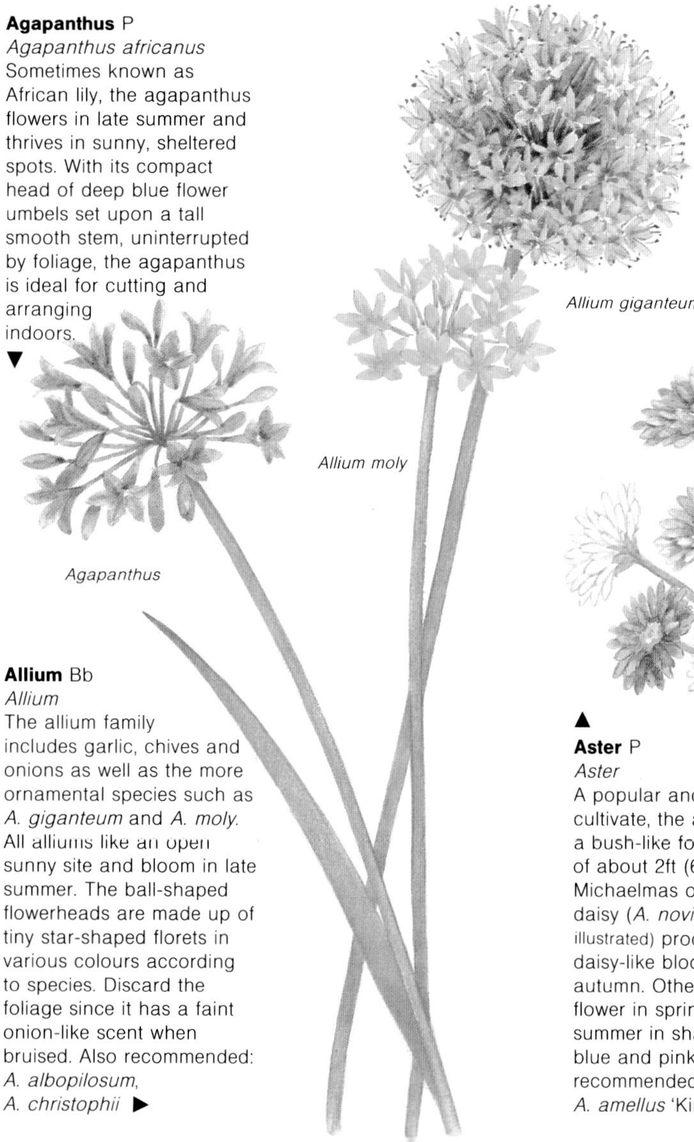

Agapanthus

Allium Bb
Allium
The allium family includes garlic, chives and onions as well as the more ornamental species such as *A. giganteum* and *A. moly*. All alliums like an open sunny site and bloom in late summer. The ball-shaped flowerheads are made up of tiny star-shaped florets in various colours according to species. Discard the foliage since it has a faint onion-like scent when bruised. Also recommended: *A. albopilosum*, *A. christophii* ▶

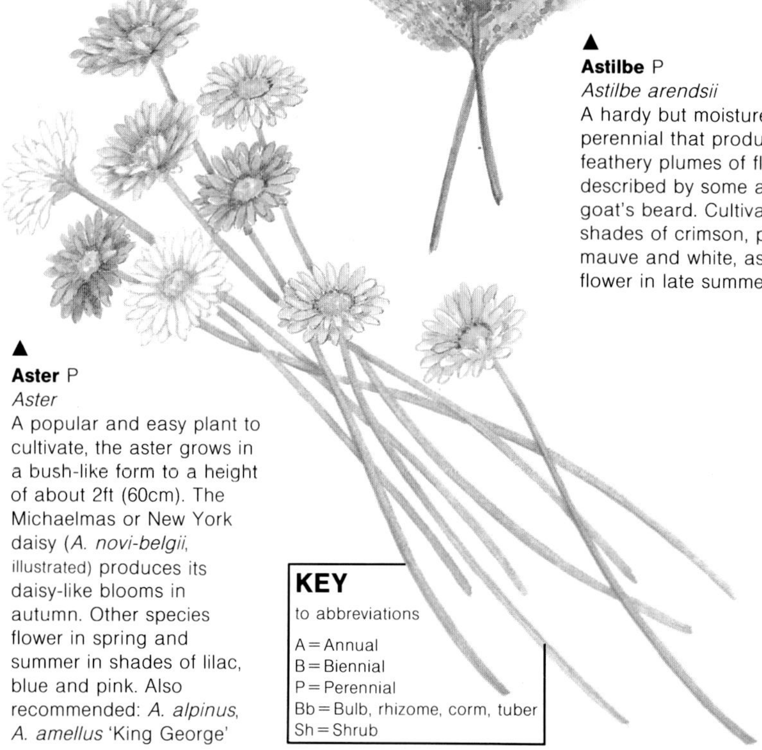

Allium giganteum

Allium moly

Aster P
Aster
A popular and easy plant to cultivate, the aster grows in a bush-like form to a height of about 2ft (60cm). The Michaelmas or New York daisy (*A. novi-belgii*, illustrated) produces its daisy-like blooms in autumn. Other species flower in spring and summer in shades of lilac, blue and pink. Also recommended: *A. alpinus*, *A. amellus* 'King George'

◀ Alstroemeria P
Alstroemeria
Although difficult to establish, once thriving in a well-drained sunny garden, the alstroemeria (known by some as the Peruvian lily) provides armfuls of carmine, orange, yellow or pink lilies from early to mid summer. Flecked with tawny tints, they look good and last well in water, growing paler as they age gracefully. Also recommended: *A.* 'Ligtu' Hybrids (illustrated), *A. aurantiaca*

▲ Astilbe P
Astilbe arendsii
A hardy but moisture-loving perennial that produces feathery plumes of flowers described by some as false goat's beard. Cultivated in shades of crimson, pink, mauve and white, astilbes flower in late summer.

◀ Camomile, Ox-eye P
Anthemis tinctoria
Flourishing in well-drained soil, the ox-eye camomile produces yellow sunbursts of daisy-like flowers from early summer to autumn. Both the foliage and the blooms combine well with many summer flowers, notably the blues and purples of delphiniums.

▲ Canterbury bells B
Campanula medium
Easy to grow in well-drained soil, the delicate bell-shaped flowers with turned up flounced edges make a ruffled appearance in mid summer. Available in shades of white, blue, purple, violet and pink, Canterbury bells are biennial and should be sown in late spring to flower the following summer.

KEY
to abbreviations

A = Annual
B = Biennial
P = Perennial
Bb = Bulb, rhizome, corm, tuber
Sh = Shrub

Cornflower/Knapweed A
Centaurea cyanus
Once a common weed, but now a colourful annual, blooming throughout summer into late autumn. Traditionally, cornflowers produce true blue powder-puff flowers but are now available in almost every colour. Cut the toothed buds and spiked, grass-like foliage and add to arrangements, as both are decorative. Also:
C. gymnocarpa

Carnation/Clove pink A,B ▶
Dianthus caryophyllus
Carnations thrive on sandy soil and flower from late summer to early winter, with frilled formal blooms in colours ranging from white through peach to scarlet. Cut the woody stems at a slant between leaf joints, not at the joint itself. Split the bottom half-inch of the stem to aid water intake, and add the grass-like, grey foliage to balance arrangements.

◀ **Catmint** P
Nepeta mussinii
A plant that thrives in sunny, fairly dry positions and flowers from late spring to mid summer, and again in autumn if dead-headed. Its tall spikes of lavender-blue flowers and aromatic grey-tinged foliage look well in many styles of arrangement.

Cyclamen Bb
Cyclamen
Planted outside in a cool, shaded corner, cyclamens will produce exquisite cutting blooms in shades of pink, magenta, red and white from summer to late autumn. *C. purpurascens* is the familiar red-flowered species, which blooms in late summer; its variegated, silver-patterned, heart-shaped leaves make wonderful tabletop decorations. Also recommended:
C. hederifolium

▲
Day lily P
Hemerocallis
An undemanding plant, the day lily will grow in poor soil, and even flower when surrounded by shrubs. Sow in spring to bloom mid to late summer of the same year. The plant grows to about 2ft (60cm) and produces sweet-smelling flowers in many shades, notably yellow, orange and red. Flowers tend to last longer than a day indoors. Recommended: *H. flava*

◀ **Dahlia** Bb
Dahlia variabilis
Dahlias are easy to grow and combine an excellent colour range (only blue is missing) with a long flowering season. Centuries of cultivation have produced an enormous variety of types. The flowers should be fully open before you cut or the blooms wither prematurely.

Delphinium hybrids A,P ▶
Delphinium
Few flowers look as good in large decorations as these great spires, which shift in tone from rich cobalt to pale sky-blue, cream to ivory or deep purple to lilac. Although it flowers for only two weeks in mid summer, the delphinium lasts well in water, particularly if the stem is crushed along the cut edge. See also Larkspur, p. 158.

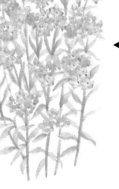

◀ **Forget-me-not** B
Myosotis
Sow seeds in summer in partial shade for flowers the following spring.
M. sylvatica (illustrated) produces long sprays of tiny, azure-blue flowers that are effective when set among the tulips that appear at the same time.

THE COUNTRY GARDEN

Foxglove B
Digitalis purpurea
Tolerant of shade, the foxglove flowers in summer with spires of bright pink, carmine, purple and white bell-like florets on a tall stem. Set them at eye-level to appreciate the delicate markings traced inside each bell-flower.
▼

Iris Bb ▶
Iris bearded varieties
Enjoying sunshine and well-drained soil, tall, bearded irises such as 'Arctic Flame', 'Dancer's Veil', 'Jane Phillips', 'Keno Gami' and 'Ola Kala' make good cutting flowers: not all irises do. These varieties flower during early spring in every shade of yellow, bronze, pink, lavender, purple and white with veining in contrasting colours.
See also pp 163 and 177.

Iris 'Dancer's Veil'

Iris 'Jane Phillips'

Iris 'Ola Kala'

Hollyhock A,P ▶
Althaea rosea
One of the traditional country garden plants, the hollyhock grows in any sheltered position to the extraordinary height of 10ft (3m). Tall clusters of ruffled flowers in shades of pink, apricot, yellow and white appear from mid summer.

Gypsophila P ▶
Gypsophila paniculata
A hardy, bushy plant that blooms into a haze of tiny, white or pink flowers set on slender stems at the approach of mid summer. Use as they are or rest them in rush baskets or pails without water to dry naturally indoors for winter arrangements.

Larkspur A ▶
Delphinium ajacis
A smaller cousin of the giant delphinium, larkspur flowers in early summer with spikes of tightly knit florets in shades of pink, lilac, violet, blue and white, according to variety.

Love-lies-bleeding A
Amaranthus caudatus
See Green Flowers, p. 171.

▲
Lupins
Lupinus polyphyllus
Easy to grow in any garden, lupins have large, fan-shaped leaves and tall, tightly clustered spires of flowers available in shades of blue, lavender, pink or coral. These can grow to a height of 4ft (1.2m) and appear from late spring to early summer.
Recommended: Russell hybrids (illustrated).

◄ **Marigold** A
Calendula officinalis
A hardy annual, the marigold produces bushy mounds of bright, golden flowers from early spring through autumn well into the winter. With such a long season it is a useful flower for adding accent colour to displays. Both the leaf and flower have a tangy scent.

Nerine Bb ►
Nerine bowdenii
This is the hardy species that flowers in early autumn. Plant the bulbs in a warm, sheltered border, since they thrive in the sun. The rosy-pink, trumpet-like flowers appear in clusters of about half a dozen atop a tall sturdy stem. These are excellent cutting flowers.

▲
Nasturtium A
Tropaeolum majus
A quick-spreading trailing and climbing plant that flowers from mid summer to mid autumn in shades of red, orange, and yellow. Its leaves have an attractive, ornate appearance, being circular in shape and wavy-edged; they are popular with caterpillars.

Masterwort P
Astrantia major
Easily cultivated from seed in partial shade, masterwort flowers in early summer. Its green leaf clusters form a natural ruff around the pink-tinged white flowers.
▼

Phlox A,P
Phlox
Popular, bushy, cottage border plant: the small blooms create rivers of colour throughout the summer. The plants are usually 1–6ft (30–180cm) high and produce clusters of tightly-packed flower heads in violet, purple, crimson, cerise and white. Recommended:
P. drummondii (A),
P. maculata (P),
P. paniculata (P, illustrated)
▼

Paeonia lactiflora

Paeonia cambessedesii

Paeonia 'Defender'

◄ **Pansy** P
Viola × wittrockiana
Since the introduction of this species, the garden pansy, many cultivars have been developed to extend the floral range in terms of size, petal formation and colour. Blues, purples, reds, oranges, yellows and whites are available on plants that flower in spring, summer or autumn, depending upon when they are sown.

◄ **Peony** P
Paeonia
A perennial border shrub that thrives in deeply dug, manured ground and produces large, striking flowers well suited for cutting. *P. cambessedesii* has a single, rose-pink flower. *P. lactiflora* blooms in early summer and is the parent of many of the most beautiful peony hybrids. Also recommended:
P. officinalis,
P. mlokosewitschii,
P. 'Defender'

THE COUNTRY GARDEN

Primula auricula

Primula denticulata

Salvia B,A
Salvia
The salvia offers prolific spiked flowers for cutting in mid to late summer. *S. sclarea* (B) grows to 3ft (1m) and produces tall bracts of bluish lilac flowers. The traditional garden species, *S. splendens* (A), is much shorter and has vivid scarlet flowers. Also recommended: *S. grahamii, S. haematodes, S.* × *superba, S. uliginosa* ▼

Salvia splendens

Pinks P ▶
Dianthus × *allwoodii*
Pinks are generally smaller than carnations. They range from pure white to deep crimson with all shades of pink in between. These modern hybrids flower in summer and again in autumn. They have silver grass-like foliage that effectively contrasts with the delicate, sweet-scented flowers.

▲
Primula P
Primula
There are many species of primula – natural waterside plants, rockery types and shade-loving garden varieties that are excellent for the herbaceous border. *P. auricula* is an alpine species and prefers a dry location; it has maize yellow, white-throated flowers in spring. *P. denticulata* produces pale lilac ball-shaped blooms in late spring.

Meconopsis betonifolia

Papaver nudicaule

Salvia sclarea

Papaver orientale

Eschscholzia californica

▲
Plume poppy/Bocconia P
Macleaya
Macleaya cordata grows to 10ft (3m), and flower in mid to late summer with tall, yellow-white, feathery panicles. Use plume poppies to make a delicate outline in larger mixed bunches. Also recommended: *M. microcarpa* 'Coral Plume' (illustrated)

◀ **Poppy** A,B,P
Papaver
The different species of poppy produce flowers ranging from those of the tissue-paper-fine Iceland poppy, *P. nudicaule* (B), to the extravagant blooms of *P. orientale* (P). To make all poppies last in water, pick them in the morning while in bud. Put the cut end in 1in of boiling water for 30 seconds. Soon the bud will split and the petals unfurl. Also recommended: *Eschscholzia* (A) and *Meconopsis* (P) species

◀ **Snapdragon** A
Antirrhinum majus
Many cultivars have been developed from this species to provide snapdragons in a wide variety of heights, forms and colours. Easy to grow and rewarding when cut and arranged indoors, snapdragons flower from early summer through to autumn.

Trinity flower/Spiderwort P
Tradescantia virginiana
This long-flowering perennial has three-petalled blooms in heavenly blue, pale lilac and white. The smooth leaves should be stripped off when the flowers are cut for display, and containers should be kept small to avoid dwarfing the tiny blooms.
▼

Veronica P
Veronica
Of the veronicas, the species *V. longifolia*, as its name suggests, has long, slender leaves and spikes of flowers in a shade of purplish-blue (illustrated). It should be planted in well-drained soil in a fairly sunny position to flower in summer. Also recommended: *V. virginica*

▲
Sunflower A
Helianthus annuus
The common sunflower, which can grow to 6ft (1.8m), blossoms in summer and early autumn, bearing massive, golden-yellow flowers with mahogany-brown centres. Not a common cutting flower and consequently one that can have great impact indoors. Check the height before buying seeds.

▲
Stocks B
Matthiola
Different strains of stocks flower in summer, autumn or winter. The fragrant flowers are cone-shaped heads composed of many highly fragrant florets. The many varieties come in a wide choice of shades and colours. Recommended: *M. incana* (illustrated). See also Night-scented stock, p. 168.

Sweet william B
Dianthus barbatus
Favourites with many gardeners, sweet williams can be sown from seed in early summer to flower the following year. With its broad clusters of tiny flowers in shades of red, pink, magenta or white with contrasting markings and spiky, green foliage, sweet william is a long-lasting
◄ cutting flower.

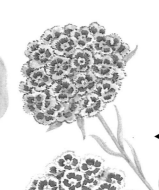

Zinnia A ►
Zinnia elegans
Like dahlias, zinnias have been highly cultivated. The medium and tall varieties are best for cutting and flower from early summer through to the first frosts. Available with differently sized and shaped petals, always densely arranged, zinnias come in scarlet, orange, yellow, cream and pink. Some strains, like the 'Californian Giant', produce flower heads up to 6in (15cm) across; others, like 'Thumbelina', blossom into masses of small flowers.

Scabiosa caucasica

◄ **Scabious** A,P
Scabiosa
Available in a range of heights and colours, including rose, crimson, salmon, lavender, blue and white, scabious blooms from early summer to mid autumn. The delicate, domed flower heads last well in water and look good with ornamental grasses and poppies.

Sweet pea A
Lathyrus odoratus
See Scented Flowers, p. 168.

SPRING FLOWERS

Richly coloured, often scented, spring flowers seem to grow brighter and bolder with the sun. First arrivals are the snowdrops, hyacinths, and miniature irises. Later come the showier tulips, jonquils and daffodils. Some spring bulbs can also be planted indoors and forced to flower in winter; either display the flowering plant in its pot, or alternatively transfer it for display to a water-filled tall glass cylinder, such as a carafe or hyacinth jar.

Crocus chrysanthus

Crocus tomasinianus

Hyacinth 'Ostara'

Anemone coronaria 'De Caen' strains

Anemone Bb ▶
Anemone
A deciduous corm which normally grows to 6in (15cm) in half-shade under trees. The daisy-like type (for example, *A. blanda*) flowers in early spring and is small in scale, which makes it useful for the town cutting garden. More popular but shorter-lived are the poppy-flowered anemones. These are forced by florists to flower in winter. The 'De Caen' strain of *A. coronaria* is boldly coloured in white, mauve and scarlet with black centres. Also recommended: *A. hortensis*

Anemone blanda

▲
Crocus Bb
Crocus
Pale blue, lilac, mauve, purple and golden yellow are the brilliant colours of the crocus flower, which blooms in early spring, carpeting the icy earth with vivid colour. The crocus grows in well-drained sunny places, or can be grown in pots indoors. Winter- and autumn-flowering species are also available.
Recommended:
C. chrysanthus, C. imperati, C. laevigatus, C. sieberi, C. tomasinianus, C. vernus

Daffodil/Narcissus Bb
Narcissus
A large genus which ranges from miniatures only a few inches high to big trumpet daffodils of almost 2ft (60cm), and in colour from white through all shades of yellow to orange. Most popular and hardy of all spring bulbs, narcissus tolerates a wide range of conditions and soils. Plant in late summer, as rooting begins early in the autumn. After cutting, the flowers may be stored in a refrigerator before displaying. Recommended: *N.* 'Beryl', 'Dutch Master', 'Ice Follies', 'Jack Snipe', 'Passionale'
▼

▲
Grape hyacinth Bb
Muscari
Easily grown from bulbs in any soil, *M. armeniacum* 'Heavenly Blue' (illustrated) spreads rapidly, hence its popularity for cutting. Small, bright blue, bell-like flowers cluster on thick stems, 4in (10cm) high, with spiky grass-like leaves.

Hyacinth 'Princess Margaret'

▲
Hyacinth Bb
Hyacinthus orientalis
Grow hyacinths indoors in shallow china bowls, patterned and coloured to go with the luxuriant pink, lilac, purple and white blooms in early winter. Or set single bulbs in special glass hyacinth containers (based on old botanical specimen jars) so that the bulb, fibrous roots and bloom can all be seen. Recommended: 'Cynthella', 'Ostara', 'Princess Margaret', 'Perle Brilliante', 'Queen of the Whites'

Narcissus 'Ice Follies'

Narcissus 'Jack Snipe'

Iris Bb
Iris
The bearded varieties popular for cutting (see p. 158) are not the only type for indoor displays. For example *Iris reticulata* (illustrated) are grown individually in peat pots, which can be grouped in a larger container. Graceful and delicate, and growing to only 6in (15cm), this iris has bluish-mauve petals subtly marked with gold. *I. unguicularis* has small, fragile flowers from winter to early spring, lilac-mauve with gold and white markings at the base. 'Alba' is a white form with conspicuous yellow streaks. 'Mary Barnard' has deep violet-purple with gold markings.
▼

Jonquil Bb
Narcissus jonquilla
The wild jonquil, which flowers in spring, is grown for its fragrant, yellow, frilly trumpets and has given rise to many garden forms. Sweet-scented *N. jonquilla flore-pleno*, the double jonquil, is a useful showy flower to set in a casual mixed bouquet; it is best suited to a sheltered position.

Scilla/Squill Bb
Scilla
A genus of bulbous plants that like any moist but well-drained soil. *S. sibirica* (illustrated) flowers in late winter to mid spring. Its brilliant gentian blue flowers sit on a stem of 8in (20cm) and can be grown as a foretaste of blue skies to come. Also recommended: *S. bifolia*, *S. litardieri*, *S. mischtschenkoana*, *S. peruviana*
▼

Snowdrops Bb
Galanthus
In all species, the globular or bell-shaped white flowers droop from graceful green stems. They grow well on both chalky and acid soils, favour sun and semi-shade, and reward with quick increase. Large-flowered hybrids of *G. nivalis*, or common snowdrop (Illustrated), include 'Atkinsii' and 'S. Arnott'. These flowers look good in small silver vases, as the sheen of silver reflects the icy white of the bells.

T. clusiana

T. kaufmanniana

T. 'Apricot Beauty'

T. 'Queen of Night'

T. fosteriana 'Purissima'

Tulip Bb
Tulipa
A large genus, tulips range from small early-flowering species to the large hybrids flowering later in spring and early summer. Lifting bulbs after flowering, and storing them until autumn, yields better flowers. Tulips are tolerant of a wide range of soils, though they mostly like sun. *T. kaufmanniana*, or water lily tulip, is one of the earliest to flower, and is parent of many garden hybrids, often with a decorative eye in the centre. Darwin tulips and their hybrids are strong-stemmed and produce large flowers in late spring. The lily-flowered tulips, which bloom in early summer, have long flowers with pointed petals curved back at the tips. In late spring, striking combinations of colours are supplied by the Rembrandt tulips – rose-red streaks on white, or yellow marked with crimson. Parrot tulips flower in late spring too, distinguished by frilled and crested petals, and by their startling colours; they have relatively weak stems. Early-flowering tulips, especially cream, white and yellow ones, combine well with daffodils and primroses, and later with the guelder rose. Scarlet tulips are effective with grape hyacinth or rosy sprays of flowering quince. Recommended: 'Apricot Beauty', 'Couleur Cardinal', 'China Pink', 'Flying Dutchman', 'Queen of Night', *T. clusiana*, *T. fosteriana* 'Purissima', *T. greigii* hybrids

ROSES AND LILIES

Roses have been cultivated for centuries, prized for their fragrant essences and their luxurious flowers. From the wild roses of Europe and the Near East – for example, *Rosa gallica* – new species were developed such as the damask and cabbage roses (centifolias). None bloomed more than once a year, and they only produced flowers in the red, pink and white range. But at the end of the 18th century, ships returned from the Orient bearing roses from China, and with these came yellow roses, others imbued with the famous tea scent and plants that flowered more than once a year. Today botanists recognize many distinct species and hundreds of hybrids.

FLORIBUNDAS

Derived from crosses between hybrid teas and dwarf polyanthas, floribunda varieties carry clusters of exquisite small blooms, although some hybrids tend to have larger flowers approaching those of hybrid teas. They bear more flowers than hybrid teas and flower for even longer periods. Cultivars popular with florists include 'Iceberg', 'Elizabeth of Glamis' (illustrated), 'Lilli Marlene', 'Iced Ginger', 'Lilac Charm'.
▼

CLIMBERS AND RAMBLERS

Climbers have longer, stiffer and fewer stems than ramblers, and often flower repeatedly, whereas ramblers flower only once but in great profusion. 'Golden Showers' is a climber with golden-yellow blooms. 'Parkdirektor Riggers' has large clusters of deep crimson. 'Albertine' is a coppery-pink rambler.

OLD ROSES

Favoured before the introduction of the hybrids, old roses were cultivated from wild roses and have remained popular for their beautifully formed flowers and heady scent. The true musk rose, *R. moschata*, has reddish, sparsely prickly stems, and flowers in small clusters of white blooms with a sweet musk scent. Most plants now termed "musk roses" are hybrids. Of old shrub roses, 'Madame Hardy' has exquisite white blooms; 'William Lobb' has semi-double, purplish-crimson flowers. Also recommended: 'Maiden's Blush', 'Königin von Dänemark'. ▶

'William Lobb'

'Blue Moon'

'Superstar'

'Whisky Mac'

'Elizabeth of Glamis'

'Frühlingsgold'

'Old Blush'

HYBRID TEA ROSES ▶

Originally developed by crossing hybrid perpetual and China tea roses. All the early hybrid teas were whites, pinks or reds, with yellow appearing in 1900 as 'Soleil d'Or'. The hybrid roses are less hardy than the older species, but make up for this with their longer flowering season, which extends from early summer and late autumn, and their magnificent, densely petalled flowers. Long-stemmed cultivars make particularly good cut flowers. 'Blue Moon', 'Whisky Mac', 'Super Star', 'Peace' and 'Pascali' are superb examples.

MODERN SHRUB ROSES ▶

Modern shrubs draw on a wide inheritance, including recently-introduced species. They tend to be tall and spreading, with repeat flowering from June to September. 'Frühlingsgold' is a vigorous shrub reaching 8ft (2.5m), attractive for its pale gold, fragrant blooms. 'Nevada' has large ivory flowers that blush pink in hot weather. 'Cerise Bouquet' has semi-double cerise-crimson flowers which open flat to show the stamens. 'Scarlet Fire' has velvety scarlet-crimson flowers with yellow stamens, and orange hips.

'Nevada'

▲
China roses

Roses imported from China have contributed more than any others to our present roses. The first China rose recorded in Europe was *R. chinensis*, although it was never hybridized to any great extent. More important was the sweet-scented China rose *R. × odorata*, shipped to Europe and the Americas, its hybrids becoming known as China tea roses. From 1810 onwards they were grown at Empress Josephine's garden at Malmaison in France, whence come many modern hybrids. There are now few old Chinas in cultivation. 'Old Blush', a form of *R. chinensis*, is a scrambling shrub rose with bright pink flowers which darken with age. Also recommended: 'Cécile Brunner', 'Perle d'Or'.

Bourbons and hybrid perpetuals

Bourbon roses were discovered in the 19th century, a natural cross between China roses and autumn damask roses. They were distinguished by their prickly stems and shell-like petals – characteristics shared with many hybrid perpetuals, which include the Bourbons and hybrid Chinas in their ancestry. 'Zéphirine Drouhin', an old Bourbon rose, grows as either a large bush or a climber, with carmine pink blooms, notable for its thornless main stems. 'Madame Isaac Pereire' is the most fragrant of Bourbons and produces large, deep pink blooms. 'La Reine Victoria' is a Bourbon shrub with pale lilac flowers, cupped like a small water lily; it grows narrow and erect.

▼

'Zéphirine Drouhin'

Gallica roses

The original *R. gallica* was thought to have been brought to Europe by the Romans. Varieties referred to as gallicas are of 19th-century origin and mostly show influence from similar groups such as damasks or centifolias. None of them are white. 'Cardinal de Richelieu' is a fragrant hybrid gallica shrub rose, a dense bush growing to about 4ft (1.2m). Buds open dark purple fading to violet as the flowers mature. 'Rosa Mundi' (also known as 'Versicolor'), which derived naturally from *R. gallica officinalis*, has deep red flowers splashed and striped pink and white. Also recommended: 'Belle de Crécy'.

▼

'Rosa Mundi'

◄ SPECIES ROSES

These are the wild, indigenous species, the ancestors of the modern rose. Most have single five-petalled blooms. *R. rugosa* has large flowers, purplish-rose to violet-carmine, and orange hips. 'Schneezwerg' (illustrated) is the smallest rugosa rose, with a long flowering period. Also recommended: *R. hugonis*, *R. moyesii*, *R. rubrifolia*, *R. villosa*, *R. rugosa* 'Frau Dagmar Hartopp'

'Schneezwerg'

The lily is recognizably the same in Byzantine mosaics as in the modern garden. Fragile, beautiful, sometimes heavily scented, lilies are often included in a mixed bouquet; just two stems can bring distinction to a group. Although many lilies can be grown from seed, germination takes up to two years. The more usual approach is to buy bulbs. The plants will rot unless the soil is well-drained. If you select the right mix of varieties, you can have flowers from spring to autumn in all colours except blue. The martagon group of lilies, *L. martagon*, named turk's cap lilies on account of the turned-back petals on each trumpet, are the best-known garden species. The Bellingham hybrids have as many as ten blooms per stem, and are among the easiest to grow. Trumpet-shaped *L. regale* has white flowers with a yellow throat in mid summer; it is notable for its fragrance. Sweet-smelling *L. henryi* is a late-summer-flowering turk's cap lily. *L. auratum* has more flowers on its stem than any other – hence, its name "Queen of Lilies". Also recommended: *L. pardalinum* (leopard lily), *L. speciosum*, *L.* × *testaceum*. A popular false lily is *Anthericum liliago*, St Bernard's lily, which is grown from seed in a sunny border.

L. martagon 'Alba'

L. pardalinum

L. auratum

L. henryi

L. regale

L. speciosum

SCENTED FLOWERS

In medieval times, small bunches of fragrant flowers and herbs, appropriately known as nosegays, were worn tied to a girdle in an attempt to improve the scent of the wearer. Today, nosegay-like decorations have grown bolder and bigger, like so many of the plants themselves, and will fill an entire room with scent. A simple bunch of wallflowers alone will perfume a room with the pungent scent of jasmine and orange that this humble little flower combines. Add strongly scented flowers to bunches without fragrance – lilac with mauve tulip, mock orange with cornflowers, eucalyptus with Solomon's seal. Some plants release a bolder fragrance indoors than out – for example, the winter honeysuckle. Others, including night-scented stocks, pinks and heliotrope, release their scent when the sun is low.

Daphne Sh
Daphne
Daphne mezereum (illustrated) is a small deciduous shrub that produces long dense clusters of sweetly scented, tiny white or pink flowers. *D. laureola*, or spurge laurel, blooms in mid winter with clusters of pungent yellow-green flowers. Also recommended: *D. bholua*, *D. odora*
▼

Bergamot P
Monarda didyma
Also known as bee balm or oswego tea, scarlet bergamot is a herbaceous perennial that flowers from mid summer to early winter. Both the broad-toothed, hairy leaves and the flower heads are pungent, and will scent your fingers when you cut them to bring indoors.

Carnation B
Dianthus caryophyllus
See The Country Garden, p. 157.

Eucalyptus
Eucalyptus
Recommended: *E. citriodora*, *E. coccifera*, *E. gunnii* – the lemon-scented, peppermint, and cider gums. See Interesting Foliage, p. 179.

Geranium A
Pelargonium
Many species of geranium have highly scented and attractive foliage. *P. graveolens* (illustrated) produces rough-textured lacy leaves that have a rose-like aroma, and flowers in summer. Other species smell like lemons, peppermint, apple and spices. Also recommended: *P. crispum*, *P.* × *citrosum*, *P.* × *fragrans*
▼

Heliotrope P ▶
Heliotropium peruvianum
Also known as cherry pie, because its bluish-purple flowers have an aroma reminiscent of this confection. Blooming from summer to autumn, this plant makes an attractive display when set with flowers of harmonizing hues.

Honeysuckle Sh
Lonicera
L. fragrantissima (illustrated) is a semi-evergreen shrub producing creamy-white scented flowers in late winter when the weather is mild. To help it last indoors, strip off any leaves below the water line and lightly crush the bottom ½in (1cm) of the stem. Its heady fragrance will be stronger indoors than out. Also recommended: *L. periclymenum*. See also Woodbine, p. 168.

Jasmine
Jasminum
Summer jasmine (*J. officinale*) (illustrated) is a vigorous climber capable of reaching 30ft (9m). Its white, sweetly scented flowers bloom from mid summer into autumn. The glossy leaves are also highly decorative. *J. nudiflorum* (winter jasmine) flowers with yellow stars from mid autumn to early spring.
▼

Lavender Sh
Lavandula
Highly evocative for its colour and scent, the species *L. angustifolia* is the old-fashioned, purple-flowered variety. The many cultivars include violet 'Hidcote' (illustrated), 'Munstead', which is stronger scented and bright lavender-blue, and 'Alba' which is white. Cutting the flowers helps to keep the plant compact and bushy.

Lily of the valley Bb
Convallaria majalis
The spring-flowering lily of the valley is valued for its pretty white bells, its rich green foliage and its wonderful fragrance. A native of woodland areas, it flourishes in partial shade under deciduous shrubs and trees and grows from rhizomes.

◀ **Madagascar jasmine**
Stephanotis floribunda
From mid spring to autumn, this evergreen climber carries starry, white, waxy flowers that are highly fragrant. These last well in water, and are effective when used as trailers in large arrangements.

▲ **Lavender-cotton** Sh
Santolina chamaecyparissus
The small, yellow button flowers that top lavender-cotton's slender stalks from mid summer are not scented, but the downy grey foliage is pungently aromatic. The scent of these dried branches is said to deter clothes moths.

Mahonia Sh
Mahonia
Truly rewarding evergreen plants for mid winter, mahonias prefer to be sheltered by other shrubs or trees out of doors but will survive the coldest winters. The scented *M. japonica* (illustrated) has prickly, holly-like leaves and pale lemon-hued flower spikes that appear in winter and early spring. ▶

▲ **Mexican orange** Sh
Choisya ternata
Enjoying a sheltered location, the evergreen Mexican orange has white star-like flowers whose smell is reminiscent of orange blossom; they appear intermittently from spring into autumn. The shiny leaves have an astringent scent when crushed.

Mignonette A
Reseda odorata
A hardy annual, mignonette was a great favourite in the last century for its scent. Its long-spiked flowers appear in summer and autumn, and are popular with bees for their almost raspberry-like fragrance. After cutting, hold the stem tips in boiling water for a minute to extend the life of the flowers indoors. Recommended: 'Machet Rubin' (illustrated) ▼

▲ **Lilac** Sh
Syringa
The common lilac (*S. vulgaris*) thrives in most gardens and produces magnificent panicles of flowers in late spring. These have a wonderful scent and come in all shades from deepest purple through pink to white.

▲ **Madonna lily** Bb
Lilium candidum
The Madonna lily – the original lily of the field – thrives in a sunny position. It can grow to 5ft (1.5m). From early to mid summer it bears magnificently-formed white trumpet flowers with golden stamens. These last well in water and have a powerful fragrance.

▲ **Mimosa/Silver wattle** Sh
Acacia dealbata
Mimosa requires careful siting in a warm sheltered position to survive cold climates. Its bright yellow, ball-like flowers appear from early spring until autumn. Arrange on a sunny windowsill to make the most of the scent.

SCENTED FLOWERS

Mock orange Sh
Philadelphus
The pure white flower clusters that appear in early summer can scent an entire room with a fragrance of orange blossom.
Recommended:
P. coronarius (illustrated), *P. microphyllus*, *P.* 'Virginal'. *P.* 'Belle Etoile'
▼

◄ Sweet pea A
Lathyrus odoratus
The humble wild sweet pea is the most fragrant of the species, and has exceptionally delicate flowers in pale shades of pink and purple. Leave it to grow all tangled in a corner of the garden and pick the flowers from early to late summer.

▲ Violet P
Viola odorata
The old-fashioned deep-purple violet, with its heady scent and pretty leaves, enjoys cool conditions and well-drained soil. Show off the beauty of the tiny flowers in narrow-necked containers.

Wallflower B
Cheiranthus
A showy plant with dark-green foliage and dense clusters of fragrant flowers in cream or glowing shades of orange, red and yellow. These flowers were highly popular in the 16th century for nosegays.
Recommended: *C. cheiri* (illustrated)
▼

▲

Woodbine
Lonicera periclymenum
A deciduous climber, woodbine (or common honeysuckle) flowers in summer with highly frgrant, ornate blooms, purple on the outside and creamy-yellow within. Cut some branches before they flower to add to arrangements, as their crimson tubular buds are also decorative.

Night-scented stock A ▶
Matthiola bicornis
A rather pallid and untidy annual, this species of stock comes into its own at night with its potent and haunting scent, Gather great armfuls of the pink and mauve flowers to bring their scent indoors.

Tobacco plant A
Nicotiana
Easily grown from seed in a sunny sheltered position, this tall annual has trumpet-shaped flowers that open and become fragrant as dusk falls. When cut and taken indoors, they do not close up during the day. Flower colours include white (*N. alata*) and lime-green.
▼

◄ Sweet cicely P
Myrrhis odorata
With its finely divided green leaves and flat umbels of white flowers, this herb looks similar to Queen Anne's lace. The plant thrives in shade on moist soil and is one of the first to flower in early spring.

▲

Virginia stock A
Malcolmia maritima
A fast grower, this species will flower within four weeks of sowing, and successive sowings may be made from spring to mid autumn. The pinky-lilac flowers are sweetly fragrant and will last well indoors if you split the fibres of the hard, woody stems.

◄ Yarrow P
Achillea
The hardy yarrow has pungent fern-like foliage and bright yellow flat-topped flower heads. As with many aromatic plants, a sunny position enhances the fragrance. Cut in their prime and dried in a dark place, yarrow flowers keep their colour for winter arrangements.
Recommended:
A. filipendulina (illustrated), *A. millefolium*

FRAGRANT HERBS

The decorative potential of the flowers and ornamental foliage of many herbs is often overlooked, as herbs are mostly grown to flavour food. Yet even in a city rooftop garden you can grow enough herbs to use as cutting plants. Herb foliage presents a wider range of colours than one might expect – purple basil, textured grey-green or yellow sage leaves, bronze-leaved fennel spikes and a range of variegated mints. The green herbs, such as shiny bay or rue, make a welcome change from the usual evergreen additions. Use sprigs and sprays with fresh cut flowers: their aromatic freshness will enhance annuals and lighten arrangements of formal waxy flowers. Try blue borage with chrysanthemums, parsley set round sweet william, variegated thyme with larkspur.

Angelica P
Angelica archangelica
See Green Flowers, p. 170

Borage A
Borago officinalis
Borage can be sown from seed in spring in a sunny position to flower in summer. The flowers open pink, then gradually turn blue. Pick them early in the season so that you can watch the transformation indoors.

Basil A
Ocimum basilicum
Sun-loving basil, a tender annual, grows broad leaves in bright green or, in the case of the cultivar 'Dark Opal', dark purple. These have a gingerish aroma and are attractive tucked into small bunches of flowers.

Bay laurel Sh
Laurus nobilis
The bay laurel is a native of Mediterranean areas but survives in more northern climates. The evergreen shrub produces fine glossy oval-shaped leaves while its yellowish flowers are relatively insignificant.

Bergamot P
Monarda didyma
See Scented Flowers and Shrubs, p. 166.

Feverfew P ▶
Chrysanthemum parthenium
This compact plant prefers a dry sunny position but tolerates moist conditions. Feverfew smells like camomile and has bright daisy-like flowers with cushioned yellow centres among fresh green leaves.

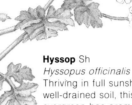

Fennel P
Foeniculum vulgare
Resembling dill in appearance but on a grander scale, fennel can grow to a height of 5ft (1.5m). Its stiff smooth stem has sprigs of finely cut feathery leaves and is topped by umbels of yellow flowers in summer. ▼

Dill A
Peucedanum graveolens
Dill has delicate feathery leaves that have a mild licorice aroma. It flowers in mid summer with large wide-spreading yellow umbels. When gone to seed, the flowerheads are equally attractive for arrangements.

Hyssop Sh
Hyssopus officinalis
Thriving in full sunshine and well-drained soil, this semi-evergreen has aromatic narrow leaves and spiked flowers in shades of blue and pink that appear in mid summer. It is much loved by bees.

Mint P
Mentha
Many varieties of the common culinary spearmint *M. spicata* (illustrated), have fragrant decorative leaves. The spearmint–watermint cross *M. piperita* has a purple stem and purple-tinged leaves; its variety *citrata* has a sharp lemony fragrance.

Parsley B
Petroselinum crispum
Easy to grow in a fairly sunny position, parsley has compact curly rich green foliage. It should be picked regularly to prevent the stems from becoming too woody. ▼

Sage Sh ◀
Salvia officinalis
A popular culinary herb with greyish-green leaves that are also available in purple, 'Purpurascens', or yellow, 'Icterina'. In early summer, masses of tiny purple flowers appear on the tall woody stems. These are highly suitable for cutting.

Rosemary Sh
Rosemarinus officinalis
This bushy shrub looks similar to lavender, but has aromatic, narrow evergreen leaves that are green on top and silvery underneath. Blue flowers appear in spring.
▼

Rue Sh
Ruta graveolens
Easy to grow from seed in a well-drained, sunny location, rue is a pungent shrub and is useful for its grey-green, parsley-like foliage. The cultivar 'Jackman's Blue' is particularly unusual for its metallic blue sheen.

Southernwood Sh
Artemisia abrotanum
This is a sweet-scented variety of the *Artemisia* family, shrubs which have always contributed attractive foliage for florists. It has fine feathery leaves and soft, greenish-yellow, button-like flowers.

Sweet cicely P
Myrrhis odorata
See Scented Flowers and Shrubs, p. 168.

Thyme
Thymus
The common species of thyme, *T. vulgaris* (illustrated), is aromatic with narrow grey, paired leaves and small, whitish or purple flowers in mid summer. Small sprigs tucked into arrangements have a pungent smell, *T. citriodorus* is lemon-scented and has larger, yellow-splashed leaves. Also recommended: *T. serpyllum*

Woodruff P
Galium odoratum
An ideal plant for the rock garden, woodruff has whorls of bristly leaves and sky-blue, scented flowers that appear in mid summer. These make an attractive addition to mixed bunches.

GREEN FLOWERS

Although Nature's predominant colour is green, this is mostly as a backdrop in the form of trees, hedgerows and grasses. So green flowers are a novelty, and quickly become a focal point. As with coloured leaves, the combination of unexpected colour with familiar shape and form makes a dramatic impact. Green flowers can be luminous and bright, pale and creamy, lemon-lime or bluish-green. Trim away foliage and use the flowers with discretion, either as part of a composition of greens, or to add accent colour to massed blooms – for example, you could use green spurge (*Euphorbia*) to prevent an armful of bright pink rhododendrons from becoming too oppressive. An arrangement of greens will be even more noticeable if you mix different tones, shapes and textures. Try contrasting the round green heads of angelica with spiky hellebore leaves. Seed heads could also be incorporated before they turn from green to brown – for example, those of poppy or love-in-a-mist.

◄ **False hellebore** P
Veratrum
Fresh green, bell-like summer flowers are tightly packed on the stems of this hardy perennial, which grows to 4ft (1.2m). Lance-like green leaves harmonize with the flower sprays.
V. viride (illustrated) is known as the North American hellebore or Indian poke. Now widely available from seed suppliers.

◄ **Hellebore** P
Helleborus
Hellebores have beautiful leaves, either deciduous or evergreen, but always deeply veined and edged with serrations, like the peony. Some also bear graceful green flowers.
H. foetidus flowers in late winter and early spring. The lemon-green, bell-shaped blooms are edged with a fine red line. The stem is also bright green.
H. argutifolius (illustrated) grows to about 2ft (60cm). Also recommended:
H. cyclophyllus

Angelica P ►
Angelica archangelica
Bold foliage on this perennial herbaceous plant often reaches 3ft (90cm) in length, so cut it for setting in big baskets. The numerous small, yellow-green flowers are grouped into large umbels, blossoming in early summer. They are succeeded by fruits which are equally useful to flower arrangers. Angelica's natural habitat is damp soil in open terrain.

Bells of Ireland A
Molucella laevis
This is a hardy annual that flowers in summer, with a large cup-shaped, olive-green calix and roundish, coarsely-notched leaves. These can be dried after picking and used in everlasting flower arrangements. In the garden, bells of Ireland grows to about 18in (45cm).
▼

◄ **Arum** Bb
Arum
A. creticum (illustrated) has goblet-shaped, scented, yellowish-green spathes (that is, leafy cloaks) that surround the yellow spadix (central spike); the flowers are followed by deep red berries. *Zantedeschia aethiopica* is the arum lily, or lily of the Nile. Mixed hybrids offer lemony-green trumpet spathes.

▲
Fritillary Bb
Fritillaria
F. acmopetala (illustrated) has nodding, snowdrop-like bells coloured jade-green outside and showing an inside edging of maroon. Growing on slender stems up to 18in (45cm), from seed it will take several years to reach maturity. Bulbs should be planted annually as they also take several years to come into flower again if picked.

▲
Hydrangea Sh
Hydrangea
Some varieties of hydrangeas can surprise the gardener in early summer with the green tinge of their creamy florets.
H. paniculata 'Grandiflora' (illustrated) is a good example: use it when the flowers first open and before they age to pink. See also Flowering Trees and Shrubs, p. 175.

Love-lies-bleeding A
*Amaranthus caudatus
'Viridis'*
Long, graceful, drooping
tassels that look like millet
are coloured electric green,
and appear in late summer
to mid autumn. Sow in a
sunny position as soon as
spring soil warms up to
avoid root disturbance, and
hope for sunshine: this
plant grows most
abundantly in the tropics.
Remove all the leaves to
show the beauty of the
tassels. Also recommended:
'Green Balls' ▼

▲
Lady's mantle P
Alchemilla mollis
The richly formed foliage
and greenish-yellow summer
flowers make this an
excellent choice for the
flower designer. The flowers
are tiny and star-shaped,
and grow in fluffy clusters at
the end of freely branching
flower stems.

Tobacco plant A
Nicotiana
See Scented Flowers and
Shrubs, p. 168.

◀ **Zinnia** A
Zinnia elegans
The hybrid 'Envy Double'
has superb chartreuse-
green, dahlia-like flowers. It
grows 2ft (60cm) tall.
Suitable for semi-shaded,
sheltered sites, zinnias
flower from mid summer to
autumn.

▲
Solomon's seal P
Polygonatum × hybridus
Resembling lily of the valley,
Solomon's seal has
gracefully slender, arched
stems, about 2ft (60cm)
long, hung with clusters of
green bells that spring from
the axils of the pale green
ribbed leaves. Inside, the
green bells are creamy-
white and sweet-scented.
They are succeeded in late
autumn by blackish-blue
berries.

Euphorbia myrsinites

Euphorbia wulfenii

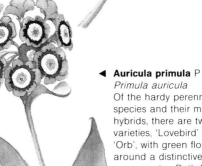

◀ **Auricula primula** P
Primula auricula
Of the hardy perennial
species and their many
hybrids, there are two green
varieties, 'Lovebird' and
'Orb', with green florets set
around a distinctive white
moon centre. Both flower in
late spring and grow to
about 20in (50cm). The
large, fleshy leaves are also
for displays.

Ornithogalum Bb ▶
Ornithogalum nutans
The white, wide-spread,
star-shaped flowers of
O. nutans, which appear in
spring, droop to show a
green banding, so that the
overall effect is of jade
green flowers. Indoors,
these flowers look good set
in small glass or silver bud
vases, so that the delicacy
of the striped blooms is not
lost, as it would be in a
mixed grouping.

Spurge P ▶
Euphorbia
E. myrsinites has slate-blue
foliage and flowers which
are coloured a bright lime-
green in spring. Easily
grown from seed, this useful
trailer looks attractive
tumbling over the sides of
an unpretentious
earthenware pot.
E. amygdaloides robbiae
has yellow flowers set
among dark evergreen
leaves. It grows to 2ft
(60cm), and thrives in poor
soil, in sun or shade.
E. characias wulfenii
(illustrated) grows 2–4ft (60–
120cm). The flowers last well
when cut.

Intensive methods of farming have made wild flowers vulnerable. You should never pick species that are protected by law, or collect their seeds, and you should never pick any flowers without the permission of the landowner. However, some wild flowers are now available commercially in seed packets, either as single species or as mixtures. The countryside thus moves into the suburban garden, and plants of heathland, grassland, meadows or woodland can be sown, grown and cut without fear of depleting the countryside of its natural heritage. This section groups wild flowers according to the habitat in which they grow.

CORNFIELD
Sow in sunny borders.

Corncockle A
Agrostemma githago
Introduced from the wild by seedsmen as an excellent plant for borders and for cutting, *A. githago* 'Milas' (illustrated) has rich plum-pink blooms with deeper damson markings radiating from the white centre along the petals. It is a hardy annual. ▶

Cornflower/Knapweed A
Centaurea cyanus
See The Country Garden, p. 157.

Corn poppy/Shirley poppy A
◀
Papaver rhoeas
The common red or corn poppy which grows in fields and hedgerows from mid to late summer is often cultivated for its tasty seeds. Pick the flowers at bud stage to watch the papery petals unfurl; but first plunge the stem ends into hot water to make them last indoors. Petals drop quickly but retain their colour and can look attractive left where they fall. The seed pod of the corn poppy will grace any autumnal arrangement.

Corn marigold A
▲
Chrysanthemum segetum
Growing to 1ft (90cm) and bearing single daisy-like flowers, usually yellow, this annual has succulent, coarsely toothed leaves. It flowers in mid summer.

White campion A
Silene alba
White campion flowers from late spring to autumn in arable wastelands. The 3in (7cm) trumpet of purest white is held on a firm stalk raised to about 2ft (60cm).
▼

Wild pansy/Heartsease B
Viola tricolor
The flowers of the wild pansy are highly variable in colour: yellow, purple and white is a common combination. Simple heart-shaped or kidney-shaped leaves gracefully encircle bunches of small flowers and last well in water. Because *V. tricolor* is low-growing, it needs to be used in tabletop posies rather than bigger bunches. See also *Viola × wittrockiana*, p. 159.

MEADOWLAND
Sow seeds in spring in semi-shade.

Cowslip primrose P
Primula veris
In early spring, two quills uncoil and flatten out on the cold ground. From this rosette springs a slender stalk that grows to about 4in (10cm), crowned with a yellow umbel of tiny primrose-like flowers. Freshly fragrant and frilled, the cowslip is a favourite for indoor displays.

Greater knapweed P
Centaurea scabiosa
Stems 3ft (90cm) high raise this thistle-like, pinkish flower out of the scrubby weeds on the chalky soil it enjoys. Agreeably, the plant has no spines or prickles, and because it is a perennial, makes an easy ornamental cutting plant, flowering from spring to autumn. ▼

▲

Meadow buttercup P
◀
Ranunculus acris
Gold, saucer-like petals surround a yellow centre of stamens and fine green seed vessels in early summer. The term *acris* refers to the plant's stinging juices, so cut the meadow buttercup with caution, wearing gloves. Widespread, deeply divided leaves at the base become smaller and simpler as they climb the 3ft (90cm) hairy stem.

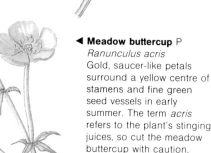

Musk mallow P ▶
Malva moschata
Deeply cut, green leaves, with a faint musky odour, are topped by rose-coloured flowers from 2in (5cm) in diameter – much larger than the common mallow. Only available in mid summer, the musk mallow flowers around the time of the first fragrant sweet peas – a beneficial association.

Perennial flax P
Linum perenne
Once grown for making the famous Irish linen, perennial flax is today mainly cultivated for its upright pale blue flowers from early to mid summer. It is a graceful plant, 2ft (60cm) high with narrow, dark green leaves and a capsule fruit which splits vertically to reveal seeds. Add it to an autumn collection of seed pods.
▼

▲
Oxeye daisy P
Leucanthemum vulgare
Oxeye always signifies a white flower, in this case surrounding a yellow eye. Flowering in late spring throughout summer on wiry stems, the daisy is a familiar sight in the open field and in gardens. Bring it indoors to add to country garden bowls. It will close at dusk to reveal the ornamental scaled, green bracts that sheath the flower.

WOODLAND
Sow in early spring beneath shady trees or banks.

Bluebell P
Hyacinthoides non-scripta
The stiffer-stemmed cultivated varieties cannot equal the charm of the wild version. Use in very simple posies.

Common St John's wort P ▶
Hypericum perforatum
A herbaceous perennial growing to 2ft (60cm), St John's wort flowers freely from early summer until autumn. Golden flowers cluster among the dark green, evenly shaped leaves. On each leaf you can see pellucid dots, the oil glands, if you hold it to the light.

▲
Hedge woundwort P
Stachys sylvatica
Growing from rhizomes, this flowering spire reaches 3ft (90cm) in late summer.

Nettle-leaved bellflower P
Campanula trachelium
The bell-like flowers can be seen throughout summer in deciduous woods and hedges. This pretty perennial grows to 2ft (60cm) and makes a fine contribution to the other bells of summer, such as the pink and mauve Canterbury bells.
▼

Queen Anne's lace/Wild carrot B
Daucus carota
Lacy umbelliferous white flower sprays make this a plant with strong decorative potential. Use it to give a lighter touch to arrangements of more traditional flowers such as roses, or tuck tight posies into small nosegays. It teams well with casual country garden and 'wild flower' collections. There are many other umbellifers, such as cow parsley, hogweed and caraway, which are very similar in appearance.

Primrose P
Primula vulgaris
Creamy yellow flowers appear in spring on the familiar common primrose, which grows on 4in (10cm) stems.
▼

▲
Red campion A
Silene dioica
Like the *Silene alba*, which flowers in white, the red species is star-shaped. It prefers woodlands and roadside hedgerows, growing to 2ft (60cm) and flowering in late spring when there are not many other red flowers to be seen.

Wild foxglove B
Digitalis purpurea
The showy, pink spikes that bloom from early summer to autumn last well in water and give a good outline to large arrangements. The common name, foxglove, derives from the flower shape, like the finger of a glove made for the fairies who reputedly, like the flower itself, inhabit shady dells and deep hollows in the woods.

FLOWERING TREES AND SHRUBS

Trees and shrubs (often clipped as hedges) provide cuttings of useful foliage as well as a range of flowers through most of the year. Happily, all flowering shrubs thrive with judicious pruning, so the gardener can reward his or her efforts by setting the results in great jars and baskets to be admired indoors. The yellow forsythia brightens cold wintry days, followed by pussy willow catkins, then flowering fruit trees with their great boughs laden with blossom. Early summer brings the scented broom and golden mimosa, both evocative of Mediterranean shores, while mid summer brings the scented buddleia, often surrounded by butterflies, and great bouquets of frothy white mock orange (*Philadelphus*).

Broom
Cytisus, Genista, Spartium
Great sprays of yellow flowers reach out from the 6ft (1.8m)-high shrub *Cytisus scoparius* (illustrated), ready for picking in early summer. *Cytisus* is the most varied of the three genera of brooms, and flowers in tawny-brown, crimson, orange or apricot. The Spanish broom, or *Spartium junceum*, flowers in late summer with pea-like flowers in bright yellow.

▼

▲

Buddleia
Buddleja
Known as the butterfly bush, the dark violet, pink or white trusses of the *B. davidii* are sweetly scented. Vigorous and hardy, *B. davidii* grows to 10ft (3m). It needs pruning in spring to take out the dead wood that has flowered. Indoors, the scent of the cut flowers loses its aroma of honey, but the long clusters of flowers make useful outline shapes in large vases.

Crab
Malus
The white, pink, red or mauve blossom on these deciduous trees is followed by autumn fruits. The common crab apple, *M. sylvestris*, has white, pink-flushed flowers. *M. floribunda* (illustrated), known as Japanese crab, is a small rounded tree growing to 12ft (3.5m), with rosy red buds that open to pale pink flowers.

Daphne
Daphne
See Scented Flowers and Shrubs, p. 166.

Dogwood
Cornus
See Interesting Foliage, p. 178.

▲

Forsythia
Forsythia
A rewarding, quick-growing shrub with flowers that spring from the slender branches in many shades of yellow. There is the pale lemon of *F. suspensa fortunei*, the canary yellow of the *F. × intermedia* 'Beatrix Farrand' and the gold of *F. × intermedia* 'Lynwood' (illustrated). Forsythia grows to about 9ft (2.7m). The flowers appear in early spring.

Bramble
Rubus
Bramble without thorns, *R. deliciosus*, has long arching branches filled with white saucer-shaped blossom, like a white dog rose. It also bears small autumnal fruit without flavour. With lobed leaves, like the blackcurrant, it makes an interesting hedgerow contribution to late summer berries and grasses. *R.* 'Tridel' (illustrated), has larger flowers, also white, with yellow stamens.

▼

▲

Azalea
Rhododendron
Spring is the time to admire colourful banks of deciduous azaleas – among the most free-flowering of all deciduous shrubs. There is a wide colour range, with particularly impressive oranges, yellows and flame-reds. Blooms are up to 2in (5cm) across. *R. quinquefolium*, with small, loose trusses of bell-shaped white flowers on spriggy stems, is among the most beautiful. Among the Mollis, Exbury and Knapp Hill hybrids is pink-flowered 'Cecile' (illustrated). The evergreen (or Japanese) azaleas are lower, and have a more limited palette.

▲

Californian lilac
Ceanothus
This small tree combines the leaf of the hydrangea with the mauve spikes of the lilac. The evergreen varieties, such as *C. impressus*, flower in the spring but will only survive in mild climates. The deciduous varieties, such as *C.* 'Gloire de Versailles' (illustrated), are hardier and flower in the summer.

Flowering cherry
Prunus
Deciduous trees and shrubs with quantities of white or pink flowers clustered on silky branches in early spring. The leaves of many species turn russet in autumn. *P. cerasifera* (illustrated) is the cherry plum, with star flowers in early spring. One of the most popular Japanese flowering cherries is *P.* 'Kanzan'.

 ▲

Guelder rose/Cranberry bush
Viburnum opulus
Grown both for its creamy white flowers, sometimes tinged green, and for its scarlet berries in autumn. Even the maple-like, lobed green leaves are decorative. A popular florist's flower, it can be grown in any soil, reaching 15ft (5m) and flowering in early summer. Recommended: *V. opulus* 'Sterile'.

Hibiscus

Hibiscus

A late-flowering shrub that needs full sun, hibiscus recalls tropical shores and the paintings of French artist Paul Gauguin, although its origins are Chinese. *H. rosa-sinensis* grows to about 5ft (1.5m) and has pink, red, blue or white trumpets set among oval, dark green leaves. *H. syriacus* (known as rose of Sharon in the USA) has rose-pink flowers. Recommended: *H. syriacus* 'Hamabo' (illustrated).

▼

Hydrangea

Hydrangea

H. macrophylla, the common hydrangea that flowers in summer, or earlier when forced, is normally divided into two groups: flat-headed Lacecaps, of which 'Blue Wave' is a good cultivar, and mop-headed Hortensia, with sterile flowers. They are deciduous shrubs with dense flower heads that colour according to the soil, growing pink on alkaline soils and blue on acid, like litmus paper.

Jasmine

Jasminum

See Scented Flowers and Shrubs, p. 166.

▲

Magnolia

Magnolia

The rewards of patience – ten years of waiting, at least – are the fine chalice cups that bloom on the deciduous *M. cambellii* when it reaches a height of around 15ft (5m). The flower measures 10in (25cm) across, is deep pink on the outside and white within. A more practical choice is the *M. grandiflora* or laurel magnolia (illustrated) – an evergreen which bears fragrant white flowers each summer, although it is susceptible to severe damage in hard winters.

Mimosa/Silver wattle

Acacia dealbata

See Scented Flowers and Shrubs, p. 167.

Mock orange

Philadelphus

See Scented Flowers and Shrubs, p. 168.

Ornamental flowering quince

Chaenomeles

These decorative garden shrubs (also known as japonica) have scarlet or orange teacup flowers in spring, followed by large, golden fruits. Most other early spring flowers are blue, white or yellow, so these plants are particularly useful to the flower designer. Recommended: *C.* × *superba*, *C. speciosa* (illustrated)

▼

Pieris ▶

Pieris formosa

This evergreen shrub, which grows to 8ft (2.5m), has creamy white panicles of flowers like a smaller version of lily-of-the-valley. In semi-shade, with peaty soil and extremes of neither heat or cold, the shrub will produce wonderful combinations of flowers and foliage. The leaves open scarlet in early spring, age to shrimp pink, then turn green in summer.

Rhododendron

Rhododendron

One of the biggest genera grown, *Rhododendron* includes both evergreen and deciduous plants, and varies in size from trees to small shrubs. Azaleas (see p. 174) are just one group of rhododendron. If you grow azaleas for spring flowers, add the early-summer-flowering series of rhododendron, the *R. ponticum* for their rounded trusses of flowers in pink, cream, yellow, purplish-crimson and red.

▲

Spiraea

Spiraea

These quick-growing shrubs have a well-deserved reputation for their abundance of flowers. Spring-flowering types (such as *S.* 'Arguta') have white flower clusters on arching stems. Summer-flowering types have pink or red starbursts: an example is *S.* × *bumalda* (illustrated), which grows to 3ft (1m). A sunny position will extend the flowering season.

◀ ## Rose of Sharon/Aaron's beard

Hypericum calycinum

Sometimes known as St John's wort, this semi-evergreen small shrub (under 2ft, 60cm) grows in dry places under trees, producing open yellow flowers among its green leaves, which are slightly fragrant when cut. Pruning improves both shape and growth. Recommended: *H. calycinum* 'Hidcote' (illustrated).

▲

Willow

Salix

Furry catkins borne on silky-grey twig-like branches in mid winter and spring provide long-lasting decoration indoors. *S. daphnoides* (illustrated) has silky male catkins, maturing to yellow over three weeks when set in water. Cut the branches of this tall deciduous shrub as the buds appear.

Witch hazel

Hamamelis mollis

See Interesting Foliage, p. 181.

GREENHOUSE AND INDOOR PLANTS

Flowers from overseas, fresh-picked and air-freighted, have revolutionized the seasonal patterns of availability. Bunches of marigolds, cornflowers and poppies, the traditional summer flowers of temperate climes, are available during winter in northern areas. But not all the flowers that defy the seasons are imports, and chrysanthemums, freesia and gerbera grown at controlled temperatures under glass make good buys throughout the year. If growing conditions are ideal, the glasshouse crop also includes some exotic blooms such as orchids. Also included in the following section are some plants suitable for growing in the home: they can be used for display either cut, or left to grow in their containers as end-stops to floral arrangements. Of course, in warm climates many of the plants described can be grown outdoors.

Camellia Sh
Camellia
Although quite hardy, this shrub is intolerant of frost, which causes its flowers to blacken in direct sunlight. Camellias are therefore ideal for greenhouse growing under frost-free conditions. The glossy green foliage is a foil for the fragile blooms set on short stems that appear in spring. Recommended: *C. japonica, C. reticulata, C. saluenensis, C. × williamsii* 'Donation' (illustrated).

▲

▼

Chrysanthemum 'Parade'

Chrysanthemum 'Tracy Waller'

▲

Chrysanthemum P
Chrysanthemum
Grown from cuttings in early spring, the greenhouse chrysanthemums begin to flower in mid autumn, just as the outdoor varieties are finishing. Chrysanthemums need reinforcement for their heavy buds, so arrange the blooms among supportive branches, or cut them down in size and float them in shallow containers. Recommended: *C.* 'Marjorie Boden', 'Tracy Waller' (illustrated), 'Parade' (illustrated), 'Mason's Bronze', 'Thora', 'Luyona', 'Solley'

Begonia Bb
Begonia
The begonia is cultivated in greenhouses for bolder hybrid blooms in scarlet, pink, orange, red, yellow and white. Remove any flowers before autumn to boost winter flowering. Begonias do not last well in water but flower profusely, so you can afford to pick them freely. Recommended: *socotrana* hybrid 'Regent' (illustrated). See also Interesting Foliage, p. 178.

Californian firecracker Bb
Brodiaea coccinea
These tubular flowers, which cluster and droop like honeysuckle, are bright red with yellow and green tips. The plant will grow in a warm location or cool greenhouse. Arrange cut flowers so that the brilliant markings can be observed at table height.

Freesia Bb
Freesia
Flowering throughout winter indoors with snowy white, pink, mauve, cream and golden flowers, the freesia is fragrant and elegant, popular for sprays. *F. × kewensis* (illustrated) is grown from corms indoors or in a greenhouse. When the leaves become yellow, lift the corms, dry them off and store in a cool place. Some freesias can be grown from seed.

▼

▲

Amaryllis Bb
Hippeastrum hybrids
Clusters of red, pink or white trumpets on a single stem distinguish this spectacular plant. The 2ft (60cm) hollow stem needs support for complicated floral art, so florists insert a thin stick into the stem to raise the flower head. Cut the amaryllis at different heights, and try setting each flower in a single-stem vase to create a line-up like organ pipes.

◄ ## Chincherinchee Bb
Ornithogalum thyrsoides
In a cool greenhouse this is an early spring-flowering plant. It can also be grown in the home, or outdoors for later flowering. The spikes of white starry flowers last well in water.

Coleus
Coleus
One of the most popular house plants, and easy to grow, coleus is valued for its variegated, usually nettle-shaped leaves. Remove flower stalks as soon as they appear. Recommended: *C. blumei* (flame nettle)

Gardenia Sh
Gardenia
An attractive shrub with creamy-white fragrant blooms, desirable for button-holes. Grow *G. jasminoides* under glass for its heavily scented flowers set among glossy evergreen leaves.

◄ **Gladiolus** Bb
Gladiolus
Best for greenhouse cultivation is the early-flowering hybrid group, *G. nanus* (including white, pink-flecked 'Blushing Bride', 'Peach Blossom' and orange-scarlet 'Ackerman'). Illustrated here is the larger-flowered *G. primulinus* 'Treasure'. Gladioli deserve their popularity as they bloom profusely and last well in water. The sword-like leaves are discarded for arrangements unless wide-necked containers are used.

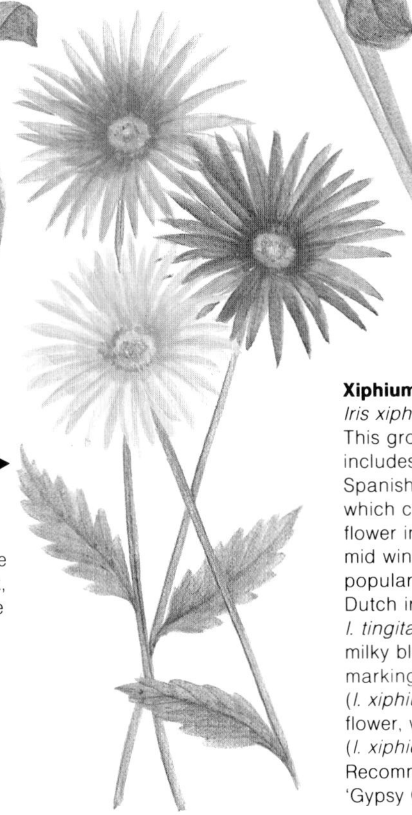

Ixia Bb
Ixia
Wiry, grass-like stems support star-like blooms in brilliant colours – red, yellow, white, vivid blue. Grow as many as eight corms in one pot and keep in a cool greenhouse.

Mimosa/Silver wattle
Acacia dealbata
See Scented Flowers and Shrubs, p. 167.

Mind Your Own Business
Helxine soleirolii
In warm, damp conditions (a bathroom is ideal) the little green *H. soleirolii*, also known as baby's tears, grows with tiny, densely arranged leaves on little pink stems. Grow this plant in small pots and stand as the end-stop to a line of small arrangements. ►

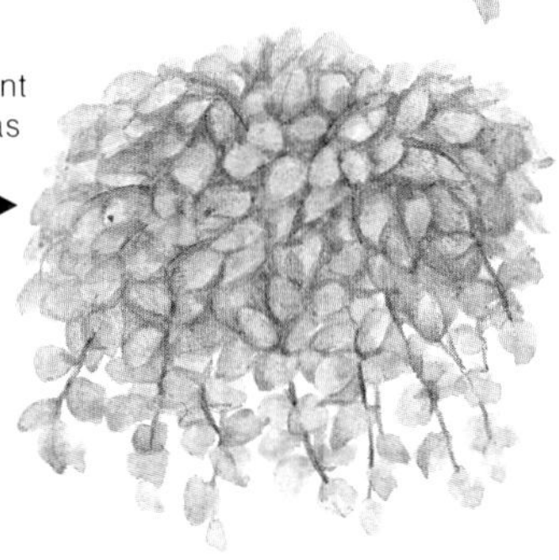

Cattleya orchid

Cymbidium orchid

▲ **Orchids**
Orchids are a large group embracing many genera. In 1836 the Duke of Devonshire paid 1,000 guineas for the *Phalaenopsis aphrodite* orchid, today grown in warm greenhouses with the *Paphiopedilum* and *Cattleya* genera (illustrated). *Cymbidium*, popular in the USA, needs a cooler environment. High humidity is essential and the fibrous base should never die out. Orchids are long-living, even staying fresh for hours out of water. Set singly to appreciate their distinctive exotic quality.
Recommended: *Cymbidium* 'Vieux Rose' (illustrated).

Gerbera/ Transvaal daisy P ►
Gerbera × jamesonii
This popular plant from South Africa has strong-stemmed semi and double daisies with crimson, pink, yellow, orange or carmine petals.

Xiphium Iris Bb ▲
Iris xiphium
This group of bulbous irises includes the English, Spanish and Dutch types, which can be forced to flower in greenhouses from mid winter to summer. Most popular with florists is the Dutch iris (*I. xiphium × I. tingitana*) 'Wedgwood', in milky blue with yellow markings. The Spanish irises (*I. xiphium*) are the first to flower, while the English (*I. xiphioides*) are the last.
Recommended: *I. xiphium* 'Gypsy Girl' (illustrated)

◄ **Nemesia** A
Nemesia strumosa
Recommended for greenhouse growing in cooler areas, this annual produces funnel-shaped orange, yellow, carmine, purple and white flowers. It grows to 9in (22cm).
Recommended: *N. strumosa* 'Blue Gem' (illustrated).

Piggyback
Tolmiea menziesii
A pretty plant of spreading habit with large, hairy, heart-shaped leaves of brilliant green. Tolmiea is one of the hardiest of all house plants.

INTERESTING FOLIAGE

The beauty of leaves is scarcely appreciated out of doors, but once cut and brought inside, each leaf can be considered for its individual qualities. Cream and white variegations; golden stripes and white splashings; plum, maroon or chocolate brown patterns in horseshoe shapes, stripes or dots – these are just some of the multitude of colourings available. Even without autumn hues, leaves have a range of bright colours – golden yellow, deep purple, tawny bronze, blue-grey or silver, as well as the various greens. Some leaf shapes will curl protectively round a collection of flowers in a simple nosegay – for example, the scalloped pelargonium, or sword-like lily of the valley. Others can be set on great sprays or branches to fill big containers. Autumn brings vibrant leaves of deep red, crimson, scarlet, gold and amber, which can be set to good effect among the evergreens and silvery silken grasses. Place large sprays in copper containers or baskets, anchored at the base with pebbles. Creepers add accent colour to a simple bunch of late-summer flowers, or can trail over the side of large arrangements. However, do not overplay these autumn browns, reds and golds. Temper the palette with an ornamental crop of berries, fruits or seed heads.

▲
Begonia Bb
Begonia
Begonia's green leaves with ornate bronze or purple markings are colourful, as well as shapely.
B. masoniana (illustrated) is marked with a Germanic "Iron Cross", while some species of *B. semperflorens* have purplish-brown foliage. Begonia leaves do not last when cut from the parent plant, but you can easily afford to replace them when they are past their best. Foliage and flowers are best displayed separately, so that each can be appreciated. Also recommended: *B. rex* hybrids, *B. boliviensis*

Artemisia/Southernwood
Artemisia abrotanum
See Fragrant Herbs, p. 169.
Also recommended:
A. arborescens,
A. ludoviciana

Silver birch/European white birch
Betula pendula
The silvery stems of the white-barked birch are hung with green pointed leaves that fall in graceful fronds. The tree thrives on light, dry, sandy soils. Male and female catkins are borne on the same tree in spring. ▶

Ornamental cabbage A
Brassica oleracea
Ornamental cabbages produce creamy-pink, ruffled leaves arising from a carmine centre. This colouring begins when temperatures fall below 50°F (10°C). Sown in early summer in pots, they will grow to 16in (40cm). When freshly cut for a table centrepiece, they have no cabbage-like smell provided that the room is not too warm.
▼

Caladium Bb
Caladium bicolor
Grown exclusively for the heart-shaped, flamboyantly coloured and marked leaves. These are mostly white, splashed with red or green outlines, but other species are plum and maroon. Recommended: 'Candidum', 'Pink Cloud', 'Spotlight', 'Exposition'

Coleus A,P
Coleus blumei
See Greenhouse and Indoor Plants, p. 176.

▲
Copper beach
Fagus sylvatica 'Purpurea'
Beeches are large, handsome deciduous trees, although some species and varieties are useful for hedging. *F. sylvatica* 'Purpurea' has glowing copper leaves that appear burnished in autumn, and last well when cut and brought indoors. The shiny green leaves of the common beech (*F. sylvatica*) are excellent for spring arrangements.

Cotton thistle/Scotch thistle B
Onopordum
The statuesque *O. giganteum* is a biennial which produces rosettes of silvery, spiny foliage. *O. acanthium* is the Scotch thistle, its tall, silver-grey stems bearing sculptured grey-green leaves, white cobwebby hairs and a candelabrum of rosy-mauve thistles. Young plants are almost entirely white.

Cyclamen Bb
C. purpurascens,
C. hederifolium
See The Country Garden, p. 157.

Dogwood Sh ▶
Cornus
Medium-sized deciduous shrubs or small trees, with glowing autumnal shades. Species such as *C. alba* 'Elegantissima' and *C. nuttallii* (illustrated) provide the most attractive foliage. *C. alba* produces rich red shoots in late autumn. The flowering dogwood (*C. kousa*) and its variety *C. kousa chinensis* are doubly rewarding, as they produce bracts of creamy flowers in summer and leaves that glow with yellow and scarlet in autumn. Also recommended:
C. florida,
C. stolonifera,
C. mas

▲
Elaeagnus Sh
Elaeagnus pungens
This variegated gold and green evergreen shrub provides year-round leaves with conspicuous markings. It comes from Japan and grows 10–12ft (3–3.5m) high. The cultivar 'Dicksonii' is evenly divided in yellow and green, while *E.* 'Maculata' (illustrated) is a deep gold edged finely with green. Florists rely on elaeagnus throughout the winter for its long-lasting leaves. Also recommended:
E. macrophylla

Elder Sh
Sambucus
S. racemosa 'Plumosa Aurea' (illustrated) is a slow-grower, but patient gardeners will be rewarded with the finest gold foliage shrub available. Elder is tough and uncomplaining. The fringed leaves unfurl copper-coloured, gradually turning to pale yellow. White flowers are followed by clusters of red berries. Also recommended: *S. nigra* 'Marginata', *S. nigra laciniata*
▼

Enkianthus Sh
Enkianthus
This medium-sized deciduous shrub, which requires half-shade and dislikes lime, has leaves that turn from yellow to flaming red held on red upright branches. The pretty, urn-shaped flowers that appear in early summer are creamy with red markings.

Euonymus/Spindle tree Sh
Euonymus
There are two distinct groups of this genus – deciduous and evergreen. The deciduous types, among them the common spindle tree (*E. europaeus*), are grown for their attractive fruits that split open to reveal scarlet seeds and their pink or red autumn foliage. The purple-red foliage of *E. oxyphyllus* is especially stunning: try this choice against a casual grouping of heathers. Among the evergreens, *E. japonicus 'Aureus'* (illustrated) is a variegated shrub, which bushes well and provides good cutting foliage throughout the year.

▼ ▲

False Solomon's seal P
Smilacina racemosa
This plant has fresh-green, lance-shaped leaves, similar to those of lily of the valley, with clusters of sweet-scented creamy flowers in early summer. The red fruit is sometimes purple-spotted. A perennial, this plant needs shade and moisture.

Flannel flower A
Actinotus helianthi
Protected in a dry spot, this annual from the carrot family provides soft, silvery-grey foliage starred with silver, bloom-like bracts. It flourishes in well-drained sandy soil and full sun.

Garrya Sh ▶
Garrya elliptica
This is the evergreen you often see set in pails in florists' shops, its glossy-green, crinkly oval leaves shaded underneath with grey. The young wood is downy. A decorative shrub in the garden, it produces silky grey catkins which make an interesting arrangement on their own when flowers are short in winter.

Golden privet/Californian privet
Lingustrum ovalifolium 'Aureum'
Many a country cottage door has been given a golden mantle of privet, as it tolerates both dryness and neglect. The yellow leaves are glossy and oval, with a green centre. Sprigs snipped out make useful year-round additions to nosegays, and the small black autumn berries contrast well. Cutting the privet will prevent the growth of berries, so leave some uncut.

Holly Sh ▶
Ilex
Anyone who has walked the holly path at Kew Gardens in Surrey knows the immense variety of leaves and variegations in colouring that this evergreen produces. The cultivars *I. × altaclerensis* 'Lawsonia' (illustrated) and *I. aquifolium* 'Argenteo-marginata' are splashed with gold and silver respectively. Bring armfuls indoors for winter bunches. The winter jasmine has the same golden yellow as green-and-yellow variegated hollies, and teams well with them when there is little colour in the winter garden.

▲

Eucalyptus/Gum tree
Eucalyptus
E. gunnii (illustrated), the cider gum, is the hardiest; it is valued for its glaucous leaves. *E. citriodora* is called the lemon-scented gum because of its fragrant leaves; it has slender white stems and white flowers. *E. coccifera*, the peppermint gum, has blue leaves, turning grey-green and narrower in adult foliage. Eucalyptuses respond well to pruning, which encourages the growth of juvenile foliage.

Everlastings A,P
Helichrysum
Although commonly grown for its yellow flowers dried for everlasting decorations, *Helichrysum* is best used for its fresh foliage.
H. angustifolium has slender leaves with a silvery down and a curry-like aroma. It thrives in well-drained poor soil and full sun. Unlike so many grey-leaved plants, it retains its silver sheen all year from cuttings rooted in spring. Also recommended: *H. bellidioides*.

Hops A
Humulus
H. lupulus, the common hop, is an astonishing climber, reaching 60ft (20m) in summer. This annual is both an ingredient for making beer and a useful foliage plant, with evenly-shaped oval leaves.
H. japonicus 'Variegatus' (illustrated) is a beautiful green-and-silver or green-and-gold variegated rambler. Hops are particularly useful for twining around basket handles.

INTERESTING FOLIAGE

Hosta/ Plantain lily P
Hosta
These hardy herbaceous perennials produce decorative leaves as well as lily-like trumpet flowers in mid summer. *H. fortunei* (illustrated) has broad curling green leaves marked with yellow which fades to primrose as summer advances. *H. sieboldiana* 'Elegans' has bluish-green leaves and white to lilac flowers. *H. ventricosa* is veined with cream on a green leaf. Hostas with variegated leaves thrive best in shade.

Lamb's ears P
Stachys lanata
Both the furry softness and the shape of these small grey leaves gives them their descriptive country name. If water is splashed on lamb's ears, it quickly becomes limp like a face flannel, losing its downy texture and its charm. Small, pale purple flowers appear in mid summer. A suggested combination is lamb's ears with white sweet peas, white roses and rosemary foliage.
▼

Ivy
Hedera
H. helix is a hardy evergreen which cloaks many an outdoor wall with its leathery leaves. Use trails of ivy as they twine naturally, never impaled in the midst of sprays the way that formal florists contrive them. Ornamental variegated ivies, such as *H. canariensis* 'Variegata', are edged or veined with gold, silver or rose. If they revert to plain green, cut them back to the first variegated leaf that appears in spring.

Lavender-cotton Sh
Santolina chamaecyparissus
See Scented Flowers and Shrubs, p. 167.

Ornamental maize A
Zea mays
Long leaves enclose broad shining ears, ripening yellow, red, brown or variegated. Gertrude Jekyll's favourite outline for blue flowers was a tall blade of maize, superbly marked with bands of grey and white and a fine edging of pink. Use in dry arrangements also.

Japanese maple/Full-moon maple Sh
Acer japonicum
This slow-growing deciduous shrub has leaves that turn a superb crimson in autumn. They are decorative enough to be picked singly to add to a mixed bunch of golden flowers. The variety 'Aureum' has golden-yellow autumn foliage. Also recommended: *A. palmatum*
▼

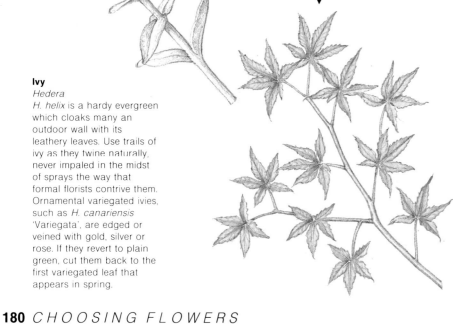

New Zealand flax/ Phormium P
Phormium tenax
With sword leaves that reach 9ft (2.7m) in length, the New Zealand flax can be trimmed throughout growth to add its flamboyant markings to arrangements. 'Purpureum' has striking bronze leaves with purple stripes, while 'Variegatum' has green, amber and yellow stripes. Hardy evergreens, all phormiums make good tub plants.

Mountain ash/European mountain ash
Sorbus aucuparia
Unlike the true ash, mountain ash, also known as the rowan tree, seldom grows more than 30ft (9m) high. Its compound leaves are made up of sharply toothed leaflets. White or creamy flowers open in early summer. Clusters of orange-red berries, which glow among gold autumn foliage, can also be used decoratively.

Sea holly P
Eryngium maritimum
This plant is worth growing from seed for its silvery-grey or blue leaves. The bluish flower head has a spiny collar. Sea hollies will last for weeks without wilting. Try mixing the steel blues with rich yellows, such as yellow chrysanthemums. Also recommended: *E. proteiflorum*.

Ornamental artichoke A
Cynara scolymus
The shiny, grey-green leaves of the ornamental or globe artichoke can be tucked into big bunches of country garden flowers. Instead of eating the immature flowerheads that develop in mid summer, use them to display indoors, as the purplish-green scales make them highly decorative.

Pelargonium/Geranium A
Pelargonium
Tricolour pelargoniums have been bred for their beauty of foliage rather than their flowers. They have velvety leaves with scalloped edges and horseshoe marking on each leaf. 'Mr Henry Cox' (illustrated) has yellow-red-green variegated leaves. Also recommended: 'Caroline Schmidt', 'A Happy Thought', and the miniature 'Red Black Vesuvius' ▶

Sea ragwort A
Senecio maritima
Also known as *Cineraria maritima*, this plant has mounds of fern-like silvery-white foliage. It grows to 8in (20cm), and should be treated as a half-hardy annual, providing truly silver leaves throughout summer. Effective when combined with white or cream flowers, especially lavender cotton.

Sea poppy A
Glaucium flavum
Also known as the yellow horned poppy, this hardy annual has silvery, deeply-divided foliage and golden flowers which last all summer before turning to ornate seed pods curved like a horn. The plant grows best on light soil and in full sunshine.

Smilax A
Asparagus medeoloides
Sprays of glossy green, delicate, fern-like foliage up to 6ft (1.8m) long are provided all year when smilax is raised in a greenhouse from seed. The roots must be contained, usually in a sunken pot, and you need to provide regular watering and fertilizer. A partially shaded position, such as the back wall of a greenhouse, is ideal.

Thyme
Thymus
See Fragrant Herbs, p. 169.

Stephanandra Sh
Stephanandra
This is an elegant shrub with pretty, pale green, triangular leaves, deeply toothed, which turn golden-yellow in autumn. *S. incisa* is the usual variety.

Viburnum Sh
Viburnum
These shrubs not only have scented flowers, but also beautifully shaped and textured leaves. This makes the evergreen species useful for foliage, while the deciduous species have attractive autumn colouring and fruit. All grow well on chalky soils. *V. davidii* (illustrated) is a widely spreading evergreen with white, flat-headed flowers and small, dark-blue berries if cross-pollinated. This is the finest species for foliage, with its glossy, leathery leaves, dark green and veined above, paler below.

▼

▲

Smoke tree Sh
Cotinus
The name derives from the wispy flowers. *C. americanus* is a small deciduous tree which grows up to 15ft (5m) and produces brilliant autumn colouring. A profusion of small, evenly coloured green leaves turn to russet, making this an invaluable garden tree for cutting sprays in autumn. Another species *C. coggygria* (illustrated), is the Venetian sumach – suitably Renaissance in its vivid 'Royal Purple' colouring, which reddens in autumn

▲

Vine
Vitis
Vigorous deciduous climbers which like full sun, vines have simple green leaves which may be lobed, cut or toothed.
V. coignetiae have large, lobed leaves in autumn shades of burgundy, claret and rose. *V. riparia* turns bronze red, retaining its green veins. *V. vinifera* 'Brandt' (illustrated) has purple leaves all summer which deepen to a rich autumnal claret. Boldly teamed with the maroon and plum coleus leaf in a shallow bowl, *V. vinifera* throws the more subtle colouring of the coleus into relief.

Virginia creeper
Parthenocissus
A deciduous climber whose leaves turn bright red in autumn. Several sprays added to informal bunches with grasses, seeds and pods give a bold colour, while single leaves can be set low into tabletop decorations. Most popular is *P. tricuspidata* (or Boston ivy), which has three-lobed leaves. *P. quinquefolia* has larger, five-pointed leaves. ▶

Weigela Sh
Weigela florida
The burnished purple and bronze leaves of *W. florida* 'Foliis Purpureis' can be picked until autumn when the leaves fall. In early summer, tubular bells of rose-pink flowers cluster on the branches. This weigela teams well with velvety-textured, purple leaves such as those of rue (*Ruta graveolens*). See Fragrant Herbs, p. 169.

▲

White willow
Salix alba
A large tree with pendulous branches, and narrow leaves which are silky-white beneath. Use in spring for its yellow twiglets and yellowish-green leaves, soon followed by catkins. *S. alba* 'Britzensis' has brilliant orange-scarlet shoots. *S. alba* 'Tristis' (illustrated) is a large weeping tree which has largely replaced the weeping willow (*S. babylonica*). See also Flowering Trees and Shrubs, p. 175.

Whitebeam ▶
Sorbus aria
The whitebeam is a deciduous tree with simple oval leaves, green above, downy grey on the underside, turning yellow and gold in autumn. Scarlet berry-like fruits appear from late summer. The late-spring flowers are small and white. This tree grows particularly well on chalky soils.

Witch hazel Sh
Hamamelis
Large, hardy, deciduous shrubs with early flowers (often scented) or superb autumn foliage, or both. Species like *H. mollis* (illustrated) shed their pale golden leaves in the autumn before flowering throughout the winter with fragrant yellow flowers, set on the crooked branches. Like a swarm of tiny yellow butterflies, these flowers bring life to the icy mid-winter scene. Also recommended: *H. virginiana*

▼

BERRIES AND FRUITS

Berries, fruits and seed pods make attractive autumn arrangements, providing contrasting shapes and glowing colours. Holly and mistletoe are well-known as traditional festive decorations. Also familiar is the pink-flowering currant *Ribes sanguineum*, with its small black fruits. Rosehips, renowned for their medicinal qualities, are easily recognizable decorative red fruits shaped like dried poppy capsules. These spots of colour, and others less well-known, combine with the browns and golds of autumn foliage. Berries can be left decorating their branches and stems, or detached and used separately, piled into small containers. Berried sprays add welcome colour and texture to winter foliage, with the bonus of longevity. Currant and elderberry supply plentiful black fruits – this is a colour not normally met in the flower world and is worth using lavishly. Pure white (the snowberry, for example) is equally eye-catching.

Barberry Sh ▶
Berberis
B. darwinii (illustrated) is a popular evergreen with shiny, holly-like leaves, yellow spring flowers and purple berries in autumn. *B. thunbergii* is the basic deciduous type, grown for its bright red autumn leaves and berries. Also recommended:
B. × stenophylla,
B. wilsoniae

▲
Cotoneaster Sh
Cotoneaster
Cotoneasters mostly have bright red berries. *C. horizontalis* has distinctive herringbone branches. *C.* 'Cornubia' has the largest berries. Also recommended: *C.* 'Exburiensis'.

Daphne
Daphne
See Scented Flowers and Shrubs, p. 166.

Elder
Sambucus
Great clusters of black berries follow the frothy scented white blossom of *S. nigra*. Gather them to garnish plates and trail gracefully over containers in the autumn.

▲
Firethorn
Pyracantha
P. coccinea has hawthorn-like white, clustered flowers followed by dense bunches of orange-red berries in the autumn. It can reach 15ft (5m) and densely covers walls as a creeper if trained.

Gold dust tree/Japanese laurel Sh
Aucuba japonica
These shiny-leaved shrubs all have handsome waxy red fruits in clusters, which last well indoors. Both male and female plants are needed for berries to develop.
▼

Hawthorn Sh
Crataegus
Clusters of white, pink or red flowers in late spring are followed by the distinctive orange or red berries (haws) in autumn. *C. prunifolia* has fine autumn foliage. Also recommended: *C. laevigata* (illustrated). ▶

Holly
Ilex aquifolium
Although the red-berried varieties are most familiar, there are also hollies with yellow and black berries.

Juniper Sh
Juniperus
The blue-black berries of *J. communis* are aromatic and set among glaucous waxy spikes. It makes a decorative branch to bring indoors in late autumn. Later, use the berries to season foods.
▼

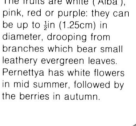

Pernettya Sh
Pernettya mucronata
The fruits are white ('Alba'), pink, red or purple: they can be up to $\frac{1}{2}$in (1.25cm) in diameter, drooping from branches which bear small leathery evergreen leaves. Pernettya has white flowers in mid summer, followed by the berries in autumn.

Mistletoe
Viscum album
This woody evergreen is a parasite that grows in tree branches, especially those of apple. The fruit is a one seeded white berry.

Phytolacca P
Phytolacca
A herb, whose purple-black berries are poisonous.

Rosehip Sh
Rosa
One of the best species for fruit is *R. rugosa* (illustrated), with hips as big as small tomatoes.
▼

Skimmia Sh
Skimmia japonica
Red berries shine throughout winter on this evergreen shrub growing up to 5ft (1.5m). As with holly, you need both male and female plants, for cross-pollination. The dark green leaves are also decorative

Snowberry Sh ▶
Symphoricarpos
S. albus has ivory berries in
autumn set upon a tangle
of black twigs, making it a
fine plant to prune and
bring indoors.

Strawberry tree Sh ▶
Arbutus unedo
Orange strawberry-like fruits
and white flowers are borne
together in autumn on this
evergreen shrub, which can
grow over 10ft (3m).

Crab apples
Malus
Flowering cab apples are
deciduous trees full of hard
golden-yellow fruits, flushed
scarlet like pears, long after
the leaves have fallen. Not
strictly a berry, but
marvellous to team with the
hips and haws of the same
season, and useful too for
white or pink flowers in mid
summer.

◀ **Yew** Sh
Taxus baccata
The dark evergreen foliage
provides brilliant contrast
with the red, fleshy,
poisonous fruit.

The practice of cutting ferns to set among cut flowers is
now out of fashion – relegated to the same status as the
aspidistra and damask rose, which were also popular in
Victorian households. This is a pity, because ferns
provide pretty foliage in many shapes and sizes and
thrive well in the steamy atmosphere in a bathroom.
They can easily be grown from the fern spores marketed
by seedsmen. Sown in moist peat, and covered with
glass, ferns can take up to six months to germinate.
Once growing, they thrive on shade and moisture. The
maidenhair fern (*Adiantum capillus-veneris*), the olive-
green shield fern (*Dryopteris filix-mas*) and the long-
fronded ribbon brake fern (*Pteris cretica*) (all illustrated)
ar partic· larly attractive. Also recommended are the
bird's nest fern (*Asplenium nidus*) and the flamboyant
brake fern (*Pteridium argyraea*), with every frond striped
in silvery down, and margined in light green. Ferns seem
to arrange themselves in graceful arches when combined in floral decorations. They look effective when
mixed in large masses in green arrangements – perhaps
with pittosporum leaves and a few green flowers such as
Solomon's seal.

Dryopteris filix-mas

Pteris cretica

*Adiantum
capillus-veneris*

Pharlaris arundinacea

Cortaderia selloana

*Eriophorum
latifolium*

Helictotrichon sempervirens

Mixed ornamental grass seeds marketed commercially
will germinate in three weeks. There is an enormous
selection, some of the best being *Helictotrichon
sempervirens*, *Eriophorum latifolium* or cotton grass,
Phalaris arundinacea 'Picta' (or gardener's garters)
and the familiar pampas grass, *Cortaderia selloana* (all
illustrated). Also recommended are: the hazy cloud
grass (*Agrostis nebulosa*) with wispy delicate
inflorescence; the tremulous quaking grass (*Briza maxi-
ma*) with graceful nodding flowers; and Job's tears (*Coix
lacryma-jobi*) with pearl-like seeds set along arched
stems. Love grass (*Eragrostis elegans*) is often recommended for use with sweet peas. Other grasses with
attractive colouring and shape are the blue meadow
grass (*Koeleria glauca*) with broad-bladed blue foliage;
Panicum violaceum with violet tassels; the reddish
foxtails of *Alopecerus pratensis*; and wheat-like
Triticum. Bamboos make effective companions to
grasses.

CUTTING AND CONDITIONING

To expand the lifespan of cut flowers, it is worth spending some time conditioning them before arranging. When you pick a flower, a skin quickly forms over the end of the cut stem. But there are various ways to slow down this process and help moisture to reach the flowers.

Pick flowers either in the early morning, when their water content is highest and before the sun saps their strength, or in the evening. Gather the most attractive blooms, but cut judiciously so as not to destroy the overall appearance of the plant. Cut the blooms at a sharp angle just above a leaf node (the point where the leaf joins the stem) so that new shoots will be encouraged to form. Angled cuts are preferable to those made straight across the stem: this way, more water-carrying cells are exposed to the water in the container. Place the cut blooms immediately in a pail of water. The water in the pail should reach to the flowers' necks. It should be tepid, as the shock of separation from the parent plant would be intensified by a dousing in ice-cold water. After picking the blooms, leave them to soak in the pail for up to 12 hours.

Florists' flowers benefit from special treatment. Plunge them neck-deep in warmer water (up to 110°F, 43°C). This will revive any flowers that have wilted. Leave the flowers in the water for 6–8 hours before you arrange them.

After they have been arranged in a vase or bowl, the life and appearance of cut flowers depend on regular topping up with fresh water. Check the level frequently. If you wish, you can strip off leaves from parts of the stems that appear below waterline: this will assist water absorption. Some people try to keep the water fresh with commercial conditioning powders. Others swear by their own recipes – sometimes adding small quantities of charcoal, copper coins, aspirin, lemonade or vinegar to the water to prevent staleness.

Heat and light accelerate the moisture loss through the pores of the plant. Flowers will literally dry out in an overheated room or on a windowsill in midday sun. Draughts also have a catastrophic drying effect. To avoid these problems you may have to lower the temperature and raise the humidity. A fine spray will replace lost water, although some plants (including lambs' ears, orchids, lilies, gypsophila and sweet peas) are ruined by water drops on their petals.

Some flowering plants absorb moisture partly through the petals – begonias, gardenias, violets and magnolias, for example. Dip these blooms completely in cold water for a few minutes, then hold them at a slant to allow the water to drain away.

Further conditioning measures you take will depend on what kind of stem the plant has. Plants with woody stems, including trees, shrubs and vines, have to work harder to feed the leaves or flowers along the branches. Beech, dogwood, eucalyptus, fruit trees, maple, mountain ash, laurel, weigela, spiraea, forsythia and honeysuckle all fall into this category. For them it is important to expose more water-bearing cells than those along the normal slanting cut. The answer is to hammer the bottom of each stem to crush the fibres so that they absorb more water. Stems crushed in this way can look unsightly, however, in glass containers. The alternative measure is to cut with a sharp knife a series of slits along the stem, up to two inches from the base.

Mimosa needs particular care if its fragrant puffs of yellow are to last well in water. Split the stems, cover the blooms in a plastic bag, and then place the stems in boiling water. Allow this water to cool before removing the bag and arranging the mimosa.

Fibrous stems, which resemble woody stems without the reinforcing bark, also need to be split and given a lengthy soaking. Examples include chrysanthemums, Michaelmas daisies and marguerites. Remove any leaves below the water line.

Flowers picked in bud have a longer life indoors. It is always a pleasure to see the buds gradually opening until they develop into full-blown blooms. I picked *Lilium longiflorum*, roses and *Eustoma* and placed them with bamboo in two shallow glass bowls and a pair of small glass jars. At the budding stage (left), the leaves dominate the display, although the delicate green of the lily buds and the four young rose blooms also make a distinctive contribution. As the flowers opened (right) they began to overshadow the etched quality of the bamboo. Colour became more important than line, and the mood changed from oriental to summery bouquet.

When arranging roses, help the water intake by removing thorns; in any case, these tend to look unsightly. Heliotropes, hellebores, tobacco plant (*Nicotiana*) and clematis last better if you hold the stems for a few seconds in a candle flame to sear the ends.

Some plants, including euphorbias and poppies, produce a milky sap which can drastically block the water-carrying cells. For such species, hot water treatment is effective, particularly if the flowers are still in bud. Place the stems in two inches of boiling water for ten minutes, keeping the buds away from the steam. Then transfer them to tepid water for several hours. If the stems are floppy and the heads droop, wrap each stem in newspaper for support before soaking the flowers. This is also a good technique for arching tulips if you prefer the stems to remain erect.

Fleshy, soft stems, found on most bulbs and corms (for example, anemones, grape hyacinths, lilies of the valley, scilla, daffodils, jonquils, gladioli and iris), need to be cut on a slant and conditioned in *cold* water. Bulbs absorb water only through the green parts of their stems, so remove the white base section.

Florists condition the hollow stems of flowers such as dahlias, delphiniums and lupins by turning each stem upside down, filling it with water and plugging the end with cotton wool. This absorbent plug will soak up more water as needed.

To improve the appearance of ferns and the leaves of ivy, ornamental kale and cabbage, vine and caladium, fully immerse them in cold water for up to four hours.

EXTENDING THE SEASON

Plants'can be forced to mature indoors so that they produce blooms and foliage weeks and sometimes months ahead of those out in the garden. The techniques involved are not difficult, and are well worth mastering to extend the season of plants that are well-suited for home arrangements.

Trees and shrubs

To brighten the barren winter months, you can accelerate the growth of blossom, leaves and catkins on trees or shrubs. It is possible to force by up to two months the flowering of scented witchhazel, silken pussy willow and golden forsythia, as well as early fruit tree blossom. The flowering currant, *Ribes sanguineum*, is actually improved by forcing, because in its natural state it produces only rather unimpressive pink flowers on a rambling hedge; but when branches are pruned and ripened indoors, the flowers that appear in late winter are, as Vita Sackville-West put it, "as purely white as any branch of white cherry."

To force the branches in this way, prune the boughs when the buds begin to swell; with some species,

such as pussy willow and forsythia, this is as early as mid-winter. Timing is critical: if you cut too soon, the buds will drop indoors. After pruning, scrape away 3in (7.5cm) of bark from the woody ends, which you should then split. Submerge the branches completely in tepid water for 24 hours. Then fill a deep container with cool water, place the branches in it and set the container in a warm, draught-free place in partial shade for five to six weeks to await flowering. Mist the branches daily. Change the water each week to assist oxygenation and at the same time cut an inch from the end of the stem. When the buds colour and seem just about to open, move to a sunny spot and arrange in a suitable container. If the flowers seem reluctant to unfurl, warm water will hasten blooming.

Foliage can also be forced – for example, that of whitebeam, beech and Japanese maple. Some shrubs will quickly replace the branches but others, such as witchhazel, take years to replace the cut boughs.

Forcing bulbs

When trees are flaunting their autumn colours, bulbs are preparing

their own yearly spectacular, putting down roots to sustain their mighty effort to flower when spring comes. However, you do not have to wait until spring to enjoy these flowers, as bulbs can easily be forced to produce splashes of colour in mid-winter, when there are few other flowers available.

You need to buy specially prepared bulbs for forcing. Easiest to grow are amaryllis, narcissus and hyacinth, which are available as special pre-cooled bulbs. Amaryllis will flower year after year, provided that you water the plant all summer on a windowsill or in a partially shaded part of the garden. Narcissus bulbs cannot be reused. Hyacinth can be planted again in the garden, but cannot be reforced.

Almost all other bulbs need precooling in the garden before you transfer them indoors to promote flowering. Plant the bulbs in commercial growing compost in pots or trays; if the bulbs are large, the tips should just peep through. Water thoroughly. A layer of pebbles at the base of the container will raise the bulbs above the water level, to prevent the risk of rotting. Place the trays or pots in a

cold frame or pit, or in a packing box in a sheltered place (such as a garden shed), and cover with leaves. The temperature should be around 40°F, although the occasional frost will do no harm. The bulbs should root in four to eight weeks. Check this by removing a pot, and tapping the underside to free the compacted earth. If the roots have fully developed, or if shoots have risen an inch above the container's rim, bring indoors to a cool room and gradually increase the daylight hours to which the bulbs are exposed. If you have no garden, you can place the pots in the vegetable compartment of a refrigerator until rooting occurs.

When the bulbs look almost ready to open, you can move them to the site chosen for flowering. From now on, give plenty of light and keep the compost constantly moist. If you wish, you can transfer the bulbs to different containers – either glass cylinders or decorative bowls filled with grey or green moss or pebbles.

Small bulbs such as crocuses, snowdrops, grape hyacinths, scilla and star of Bethlehem are all easy to force. Tulips can be forced but need careful temperature control.

GLOSSARY / BIBLIOGRAPHY

Words in CAPITAL LETTERS denote cross-references.

Annual A plant with a whole lifespan, from seed to flowering and death, of a year – or usually considerably less.

Axil The angle or junction between a stem and a leaf growing from it. The bud within the angle is described as axillary.

Basal leaves The lowest leaves of a plant, arising at or near soil level, often of different shapes from those on the stem.

Bedding plants Plants which are put in place in the garden for one season only – as opposed to border plants which are permanent. They may be ANNUALS or BIENNIALS, or tender plants borrowed from the greenhouse.

Biennial A plant that completes its life-cycle in two growing seasons, forming a leafy plant in the first year, then flowering and seeding in the second year before dying.

Bract A leaf or leaf-like structure that protects the flowers as it forms. Bracts occur at the base of a flower stalk or at the stem of a flower cluster; or, as in COMPOSITE plants, they form part of the flower head itself.

Bulb A bulb is a modified bud, usually formed underground, with fleshy scales or swollen leaf bases which store food during a rest period. The term is commonly used for all flowers with this or similar modes of growth. See also CORM, RHIZOME, TUBER.

Calyx The SEPALS or outermost ring of modified leaves that form a flower. They are usually green and inconspicuous but may look just like petals (as in clematis) or replace them.

Carpel A single female unit of a flower, usually composed of a *stigma*, on which pollen lands, a *style* down which a pollen tube grows and an *ovary* in which fertilization takes place.

Catkin A dense spike of petalless, usually unisexual, flowers often, but not invariably, pendent and wind-pollinated. Male and female catkins often look very different, as in many willows (*Salix*), where the males, covered with yellow pollen, are much the prettier.

Composite Any of the species in the daisy family Compositae, including chrysanthemums and zinnias. The flowers are made up of tightly grouped small flowers (FLORETS), either tubular or strap-shaped.

Corm A swollen underground stem base which stores food reserves. Unlike a BULB, a corm is not layered, but the whole is covered with papery scales. Gladiolus and crocus are among the most common examples.

Cultivar Short for "cultivated variety", cultivar is the correct term for what most gardeners know as a "variety" – that is, a horticulturally selected plant.

Dead-heading Removing faded flowers from a plant, partly for its appearance but also to prevent it from spending its energy on producing seeds. Dead-heading often produces, as in rhododendrons, a better crop of flowers the following year, or, as in perpetual-flowering roses and many herbaceous plants (especially annuals), it encourages more flowers to grow.

Deciduous A term applied to a plant that loses all its leaves at one time of year, usually late autumn.

Division The deliberate separation of a clump-forming plant into two or more parts as a means of propagation.

Double Flower with more than the usual complement of petals. In a double flower some of the sexual organs (stamens or carpels) are transformed into petals.

Family A group of plant GENERA sharing a set of basic characteristics such as flower composition. Most family names end in -aceae, but there are exceptions, such as Compositae (daisies) and Graminae (grasses).

Fern A non-flowering plant that reproduces by means of spores borne on the underside of leaf-like fronds.

Fertilization The fusion of male and female sex cells. If pollen and female cell are on the same plant, then *self-fertilization* can occur; otherwise, *cross-fertilization* takes place.

Floret Any of the small individual flowers making up a COMPOSITE flower such as a daisy.

Floribunda Literally, the term means having lots of flowers. Floribunda roses are modern cluster-flowering bushes closely related to HYBRID TEAS.

Forcing The act of hurrying plants into maturity by artificial means, usually by raising the temperature.

Genus A group of plants with common characteristics agreed by botanists probably to have evolved from a common ancestor. Each genus is comprised of one or more SPECIES, and is denoted by the first part of a plant's Latin name.

Germination The emergence of a plant from a seed.

Glaucous Term used to describe a blue or grey-green leaf or fruit.

Hardy Term describing a plant that is capable of surviving the whole of its lifespan without any form of protection against fluctuations of weather.

Herb Any non-woody, non-shrubby plant. However, the term is usually applied specifically to aromatic plants used for culinary flavouring.

Hybrid A plant resulting from cross-breeding between two different SPECIES, true-breeding VARIETIES or GENERA. Hybrids are sometimes sterile and never true-breeding. They are denoted by the sign × as in *Chaenomeles × superba*.

Hybrid tea The typical modern bedding rose, with one flower to a stem, derived by elaborate breeding from the tea roses of China.

Inflorescence The arrangement of flowers on the stem.

Palmate Adjective describing a leaf shaped like an open hand.

Panicle A branched flower head with groups of stalked flowers. Lilacs are common examples.

Perennial A plant that lives for more than two years.

Perpetual A term used of roses that flower more than once each year.

Pruning The removal of stems, branches or roots of a tree or shrub. Pruning is performed to alter plant shape, to increase vigour, to remove dead or damaged parts or to help improve the quantity and quality of flowers and fruits.

Raceme An elongated, unbranched flower head or (inflorescence) bearing short-stalked flowers. The top of the inflorescence continues to grow and produce new buds as the lower flowers open.

Rhizome A swollen, creeping underground stem bearing roots, leafy shoots and flowering stems. A rhizome is an organ of storage and, for the gardener, of propagation. Bearded irises are a common example.

Semi-double A flower with more than the usual complement of petals but not a full DOUBLE.

Sepal One of the outer ring of modified leaves forming the CALYX of a flower.

Shrub Any plant with many woody stems, the main ones usually arising from near the base.

Spadix A fleshy, elongated flower head in which small, insignificant flowers are embedded in pits. The spadix is normally sheathed in a SPATHE.

Spathe A modified leaf often found wrapped like a cloak around a SPADIX, as in the arum family.

Species A group of mutually fertile plants sharing essential characteristics that are distinctive and breed true from generation to generation. Details such as petal colour and leaf shape may vary between individuals. Each species is given a two-word Latin name; in *Viola biflora*, for example, *Viola* is the GENUS name, *biflora* the species. Plants with persistent-ly different detailed structures may be grouped into sub-species or varieties.

Spike An elongated flower head (inflorescence) in which stalkless flowers occur. The flower head is unbranched and the lower flowers open first.

Sterile Describes any plant that bears no viable sex cells, seeds or fruits. HYBRIDS are often sterile.

Truss A cluster of flowers or fruits.

Tuber A swollen plant stem or root, usually found underground. Tubers contain stored food. In stem tubers, such as dahlias, new growth arises from the attached stem or crown.

Umbel A flower head in which flowers are borne on stalks arising from a single point on the stem like the spokes of an umbrella.

Variegated Term used to describe plants with yellow, cream or white markings on their leaves due to an absence of chlorophyll – the green pigment which absorbs light.

BIBLIOGRAPHY

Gault, S. Millar and Patrick M. Synge, *The Dictionary of Roses in colour*, Ebury Press and Michael Joseph (in collaboration with the Royal Horticultural Society and the Royal National Rose Society), London 1971

Hay, Roy and Patrick M. Synge, *The Dictionary of Garden Plants in colour* (in collaboration with the Royal Horticultural Society), London 1969

Hobhouse, Penelope, *Colour in Your Garden*, Collins, London 1985

Jekyll, Gertrude, *Colour in the Flower Garden*, Country Life, London

Johnson, Hugh, *The Principles of Gardening*, Mitchell Beazley, London 1979 and Simon and Schuster, New York 1979

Otis, Denise, with Ronaldo Maia and Ernst Beadle, *Decorating with Flowers*, Abrams, New York 1978

Verey, Rosemary, *The Scented Garden*, Michael Joseph, London 1981

Vita Sackville-West's Garden Book, Michael Joseph, London 1968

Wright, Michael, *The Complete Handbook of Garden Plants*, Michael Joseph/Rainbird, London 1984

INDEX OF PLANTS

Page numbers in **bold** refer to captions and illustrations.

ACKNOWLEDGMENTS

The Author and Publishers would like to thank the following for their generous help in producing this book:

For horticultural advice: Evelyn Shearer and June Wade of the florists Pulbrook and Gould, London
For help with locations: Robin Guild; Judith and Martin Miller; Next Interior; Designers Guild

Thanks are also due to *Cosmopolitan* magazine for their permission to reproduce the photographs of Tricia Guild's house on pages 128–9

Fabrics from Designers Guild

Ceramists' work shown in the photographs includes:
13 Ivo Mosley (top)
29 Emmanuel Cooper
44 Jane Forster dish and Jacques Molin vase (left)
44 Jacques Molin vases
46 Judy Caplin
56 Janice Tchalenko
57 Karen Bunting
59 Janice Tchalenko (bottom)
64 Carol McNichol (left)
64 Suzanne Bergne (top)
65 Suzanne Bergne
67 Janice Tchalenko (right)
70 Emmanuel Cooper
78 Ivo Mosley (left)
79 Pots by Karen Bunting
98–9 Hinchcliffe and Barber
103 Sebina Teuteberg
115 Janice Tchalenko (right)
147 Jacques Molin vases, Emmanuel Cooper bowl
152 Janice Tchalenko (left)